WINDSOR
AND THE GREAT PARK
A COMPANION GUIDE

MIKE COPE

Dedication

To the memory of my father
Francis John Cope ('Jack') 1926–2018
and
Richard Cope 1824–1912
Chapter Clerk of St George's Chapel,
Windsor Castle

First published in Great Britain in 2019

Text and images © Mike Cope 2019, except where indicated in the captions.

British Library Cataloguing-in-Publication Data
A CIP record for this title is available from the British Library

ISBN 978 0 85710 124 2

PiXZ Books
Halsgrove House, Ryelands Business Park,
Bagley Road, Wellington, Somerset TA21 9PZ
Tel: 01823 653777
Fax: 01823 216796
email: sales@halsgrove.com

An imprint of Halstar Ltd, part of the Halsgrove group of companies.
Information on all Halsgrove titles is available at:
www.halsgrove.com

Printed and bound in India by
Parksons Graphics

CONTENTS

INTRODUCTION

It has been said that Windsor Castle provides the image most people would associate with the idea of England.[1] It ranks on a par with Buckingham Palace, St Paul's Cathedral and the Houses of Parliament as an icon of the Empire. Standing high on its elongated chalk ridge, the cluster of towers, turrets and crenelated battlements, crowned by the Round Tower, provides a breath-taking vista when viewed from the railway arch over the Clewer footpath or the Eton Brocas. Up Thames Street, where the castle is wedded to the town, the cliff-life walls dwarf the town shops and give the fortress a sense of scale. In the centre of town, near Castle Hill and King Henry VIII Gate, the crowds are perhaps the thickest – especially when the guard is being changed. A view from the Long Walk towards the South Front – the Regency fantasy conceived by King George IV – is one of the grandest: either from the monument on Snow Hill or closer in, where the Albert Road from Old Windsor bisects the avenue. A glimpse from a railway carriage or a sideways glance from a car window, hurtling along the A332 dual carriageway from Slough, is another viewpoint. Leaving on a plane out of Heathrow offers a modern aerial perspective: the Wraysbury gravel pits flying past, the Long Walk's unmistakable line of trees, the Castle precincts laid out below like a model village - then into the clouds. A hundred years ago, the poet Edward Thomas[2] described the view of Windsor Castle from the meadows of Clewer, as rising *'like a cloud in the east, with nothing behind, or on either side of it, but a sky of dull silver, and nothing below but the smoke wreaths of the town gently and separately ascending'*.

A view from a high balcony on the High Street looking towards Queen Victoria's Statue during Guard Mount.
© *Doug Harding.*

View of the South Front of Windsor Castle from Snow Hill at the start of the 2018 Windsor Half Marathon.

The band of the Household Calvary file past Queen Victoria's Statue as they return to barracks.

The Coat of Arms of New Windsor featuring the Royal Standard of Edward I and the castle motif of his Queen, Eleanor of Castile. Edward I granted New Windsor its first Borough charter on 28 May 1277.

The origin of the name 'Windsor' (or Windlesora) has given rise to much speculation. One suggestion is that it means a 'riverbank with a windlass'. Another is that the first part of the word represents the name of a local Saxon chief, Waendle[3] and the second half is a common ending in the neighbourhood meaning 'dwelling' or 'weir'. A further suggestion is that the name is derived from the winding shore of the river at this point.

The scope of this companion guide is intentionally broad, and covers not only Windsor Castle, but the relationship between the urban community of Windsor and the Royal one. Chapters on the Great Park, Windsor Town, Windsor Events, Literary Windsor and the River Thames examine this theme further. For those who wish to explore the area on foot, four walks (between 1 and 8 miles) are also included. With over 190 illustrations, including drone and aerial photographs, alongside conventional images, this companion guide paints a picture of a Royal town steeped in history, pageantry and heritage.

Books and websites used for researching this companion guide are acknowledged in a detailed Notes section at the end of the book. They also provide the reader with ample opportunity for further reading.

Bronze statue of Queen Victoria erected in 1887 to commemorate her Golden Jubilee.

CHAPTER 1

WINDSOR CASTLE — A TOUR OF THE PRECINCTS

'It is the most romantique castle that is in the world.'
Samuel Pepys, 1666

Windsor is best known for its castle – home to the British monarchy for over 900 years, and the largest inhabited castle in the world. Only 25 miles from London and 10 miles from Heathrow Airport, the castle attracts over a million visitors a year, and is an official residence of the reigning Monarch. As well as a royal palace, the castle also contains a collegiate church and the homes and workplaces of around 200 people, including the Military Knights of Windsor and the Dean and Canons of St George's Chapel[1]. The castle is used for ceremonial and state occasions, including state visits from overseas monarchs and presidents. HM The Queen spends most of her private weekends at Windsor Castle and takes up official residence for a month in the Spring for Easter Court and a week in June for Royal Ascot and the Order of the Garter service[2]. In a 'Letter to a Noble Lord', in 1796, Edmund Burke compared the British Monarchy to *'the proud keep of Windsor'* and over 200 years later, the saying is still as apt.

View of Windsor Castle from the Great Park — looking majestic in the June sunshine.

Drone photograph of the Thames and Windsor Castle taken from high above The Brocas. © *Doug Harding*.

View of Windsor Castle and The Long Walk taken from Snow Hill during Royal Ascot week.

The Saxon kings held court at Old Windsor, just a few miles down river, in an ancient settlement called Windlesora, but it was not until the eleventh century that William the Conqueror, after his victory at Hastings, built his first fortress in London (the White Tower) and then surrounded it with a ring of nine castles[3], about 25 miles apart from each other and within a day's march of the city. The steep chalk bluff on the banks of the Thames, near Clewer, was the obvious place to build a fortress (to defend the western approach to London), and the modern town of new Windsor grew up around the original motte, keep and wooden palisade that William the Conqueror erected there. Easy access to London (via The Thames) and the proximity of a royal hunting forest also recommended it as a royal residence for future kings.

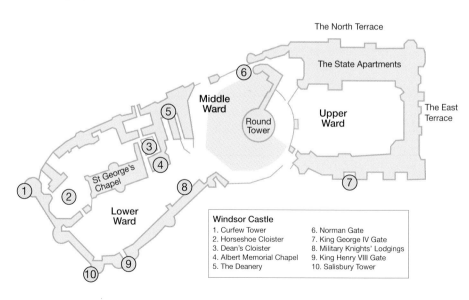

The North Terrace

The State Apartments

⑥

Middle Ward

⑤

Round Tower

Upper Ward

The East Terrace

③

④

St George's Chapel

⑧

⑦

①

②

Lower Ward

⑨

⑩

Windsor Castle

1. Curfew Tower
2. Horseshoe Cloister
3. Dean's Cloister
4. Albert Memorial Chapel
5. The Deanery

6. Norman Gate
7. King George IV Gate
8. Military Knights' Lodgings
9. King Henry VIII Gate
10. Salisbury Tower

The Middle Ward and The Round Tower

Crowning the Middle Ward is the Round Tower, Windsor's famous landmark, visible for miles around. It was built as the main stronghold of the castle by King Henry II in the twelfth century[4] on a mound raised by William the Conqueror and has stood guard over Windsor Castle for over 800 years. The mound (or motte) is the oldest part of the castle and is made from chalk excavated from the surrounding ditch. It was originally topped by a wooden keep. King Edward III was the first king to turn Windsor Castle into a palace and royal residence, spending £50,000 in the currency of his time during the transformation process. In 1343, inspired by the Arthurian legend, he hosted a Round Table at Windsor[5] for his new Order of the Garter, and two years later commanded a circular stone building, 200 feet in diameter, to be erected in the upper bailey to house his Round Table. Later in the nineteenth century, King George IV (and his architect Sir Jeffry Wyatville) increased the height of the Round Tower by around 30 feet and added a flag turret.[6]

The shape of the Round Tower is not strictly round, but rather D-shaped with a flattened southern flank. The Barons, who were hunting King John, badly damaged one side of the castle during the 1216 siege and the subsequent repairs have left it with a flattened wall ever since.

The ceremonial Royal Standard flies over Windsor Castle to celebrate Garter Day. This immense flag (about the size of a double-decker bus) measures 38 feet across by 19 feet deep and flies only on very special occasions. At other times a smaller version of the Royal Standard is flown, when the monarch is in residence. The flag is split into four quadrants: top left and bottom right represent England, featuring three gold lions on a red field; top right represents Scotland and features a red lion rampant on a gold field; bottom left represents Ireland and features a gold harp on a blue field. © *Doug Harding*.

The Norman Gate, an inner gatehouse with cylindrical towers, was built in 1357 by William of Wykeham, Bishop of Winchester. It is the principal access to the Upper Ward and also guards the stairway leading up to the Round Tower. © *Doug Harding*.

Visitors to Windsor Castle can join a 'Conquer the Tour' tour[7] during the summer months, and climb the 200 steps to the top of the Round Tower, which is 65.5 metres above the River Thames. The first stop on the 'Conquer the Tower' tour is a visit to the external 'gallery' at the base of the tower's drum, which is equipped with sixteen 18th-century bronze field guns mounted on cast-iron carriages. There are fine views here over The Quadrangle to The Queen's Private Apartments. You can also view the tower's walls, built with heath stone from nearby Bagshot Heath, and see the galletting in the stonework (chips of flint in the mortar). When you reach the top, your efforts are rewarded with panoramic views across Windsor Great Park, the Thames Valley, and the London skyline, as well as across the other castle precincts. The tour also provides a close-up view of the castle's 15-metre flagpole, made from the trunk of a Canadian Douglas Fir, which flies the Royal Standard when the reigning monarch is in residence and the Union Flag at other times. When the current flagpole was first raised in 1892, workmen buried a box containing coins beneath it. This follows the naval tradition of 'mast stepping', when coins were placed below the main mast of a ship, so that any sailor who lost his life at sea could pay the ferryman of Greek mythology to row him across the River Styx and into the afterlife.[8]

The Round Tower is also home to the Royal Archives – a unique collection of documents relating to the history of the British Monarchy over the last 250 years.[9] The personal and official correspondence of monarchs from King George III onwards, as well as administrative records of the departments of the Royal Household, are preserved here.

View of the Round Tower from Castle Hill, near the visitor entrance area.

Aerial panorama of the State Apartments and the Quadrangle in the Upper Ward, Windsor Castle. The Quadrangle is the perfect setting for many colourful ceremonies, including state visits. Here the foreign head of state can inspect the Guard of Honour, before watching the military march past. To the upper left of the picture is the East Terrace Garden — a superb Italian-style garden, complete with terraces, fountain and orangery, which was created by King George IV on an exposed east-facing hilltop. This was achieved by enclosing it within a raised stone wall, whose top was level with the terraces — giving it an appearance of a sunken garden, and protecting it from the keen east winds. © *Jason Hawkes*.

The Upper Ward and The State Apartments

The medieval expansion of Windsor took place under King Edward III when the castle was converted into a Gothic palace.[10] Reconstruction of the Upper Ward began in 1357 under the direction of the Clerk of Works, William of Wykeham, Bishop of Winchester. An inner gatehouse was built with cylindrical towers (the 'Norman Gate') as the principal entrance to the Upper Ward. Along the south side facing the Quadrangle, the Great Hall and Royal Chapel were built. King Edward III's State Apartments survived until the seventeenth century, hardly altered by later medieval kings. On the restoration of the monarchy in 1660, King Charles II set out to reinstate Windsor as his main non-metropolitan residence. The walls of the State Apartments were panelled in oak and festooned with limewood carvings by Grinling Gibbons and his assistant Henry Phillips. The carved fruit and flowers, crabs and lobsters form a graceful series of ornaments, enhancing the fine pictures which throng the State Apartments.[11] John Evelyn, the diarist, stumbled on Gibbons' carving talent purely by chance, as he explains in his diary entry of 18 January 1671:

> *Of this young artist, together with my manner of finding him out, I acquainted the King, and begged that he would give me leave to bring him and his work to Whitehall. This was the first notice his Majesty ever had of Mr. Gibbon.*[12]

Wren and Evelyn introduced Gibbons to King Charles II who gave him his first commission, which is still residing in the dining room of Windsor Castle. The copper statue of the king on horseback, on its marble pedestal with carved relief, is also the work of Gibbons. Antonio Verrio, an Italian artist brought to Windsor from Paris, was responsible for creating the exquisite painted ceilings. Only those in the Queen's Presence and Audience Chambers and the King's Dining Room have survived, but the general form and proportion of the State Apartments today are still as created by King Charles II. In his reign, the North Terrace was also extended around the outside of the east and south sides of the Quadrangle.[13]

The first two Georges appeared to neglect the castle, but King George III chose it as his favourite residence and after his recovery from his first attack of

The north face of Windsor Castle viewed from the playing fields of St George's School. This area of the Home Park is out of bounds to the public — except on special occasions, such as the Royal Windsor Horse Show.

porphyria in 1789, decided to move to Windsor.[14] He converted the round-arched windows to the more fashionable Gothic style, and lightened the appearance of the state rooms by replacing the oak panelling with coloured fabrics. In addition a new state entrance and Gothic staircase were constructed.

Snow enfolds the grounds of The Home Park leading to King George IV Gate. © *Doug Harding*.

The southern approach to Windsor Castle viewed from the Long Walk — with the double avenue of trees bedecked in autumn livery.

When his son, King George IV, ascended the throne he continued the Gothic transformation of the castle, chiefly influenced by his artistic advisor Sir Charles Long. Three leading architects were asked to submit plans and also James Wyatt's nephew, Jeffry, who was awarded the commission. Some of his main achievements were the enhancement of the silhouette of the castle, with additional towers and battlements, the inclusion of a Grand Corridor around the Upper Ward and the continuation of the Long Walk up to the castle culminating in the King George IV Gate.[15] Wyatt carried out Long's programme to the last detail earning a knighthood for himself and medievalising his surname to Wyatville. A nineteenth century wag couldn't resist the following epigram[16]:

> *Let George, whose restlessness leaves nothing quiet,*
> *Change if He must the good old name of Wyatt;*
> *But let us hope that their united skill*
> *Will not make Windsor Castle Wyatt Ville.*

The Garter Throne Room was also created by Wyatville and it is in this room that the Sovereign invests new Knights and Ladies of the Garter with the insignia of the Order, before their installation in St George's Chapel on Garter Day. Sir Jeffry Wyatville took up residence in the Winchester Tower in 1824 and is buried in St. George's Chapel (his memorial stone is sited in the north-east corner behind the high altar).[17] It was probably the greatest work of King George IV to make Windsor Castle *'as young as the Brighton Pavilion'.*[18]

To enter the newly refurbished State Apartments, the visitor must ascend the imposing Grand Staircase, which is dominated by a huge marble statue of King George IV - the monarch largely responsible for the present appearance of the castle. But it was King Charles I who amassed an art collection to rival all others and assembled one of the most extraordinary art collections of his age, including works by Van Dyck and Rubens. After his execution outside the Banqueting House in Whitehall Palace on 30 January 1649, the exceptional masterpieces were sold off piecemeal by Oliver Cromwell to raise funds and pay off Charles's debts. Some of these were retrieved by King Charles II during the Restoration and the Van Dyck family portraits are now displayed in the Queen's Ballroom[19]. (The triple portrait of King Charles I, showing the King in three positions, is displayed in the adjoining room – the Queen's Drawing Room.) In 2018, an exhibition at the Royal Academy[20] reunited the greatest masterpieces from this legendary collection for the first time – over 100 works of art, ranging from classical sculptures and Baroque paintings to exquisite miniatures and monumental tapestries.

Another room designed by Wyatville was The Waterloo Chamber, which was created to celebrate the Allied victory over Napoleon in 1815, and to display commissioned portraits (by Sir Thomas Lawrence) of allied monarchs, statesman and commanders who contributed to Wellington's victory. The room also plays host to the Garter Luncheon, which is given by HM The Queen to the Companions of the Garter each June.

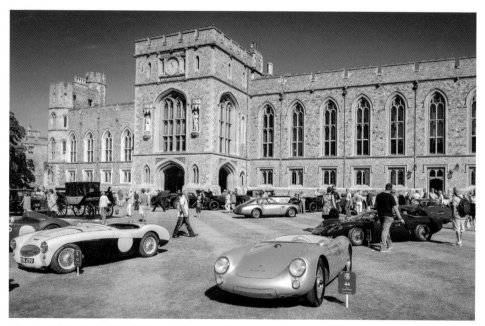

A Porsche 550 Spyder (built in 1955) on display at the Concours of Elegance event, Windsor Castle, in 2012. Only ninety 550s were produced, each featuring a super lightweight aluminium body, with two seats and an open-top.
© Doug Harding.

On 20 November 1992 a devastating fire swept through the State Apartments. It broke out in Queen Victoria's private chapel (now re-named The Lantern Lobby) in the north-east corner of the Upper Ward. It is thought to have been caused by a workman's spotlight igniting a curtain high above the altar.[21] The fire spread rapidly at roof level and severely damaged the ceilings of St George's Hall and the Grand Reception Room, as well as gutting the Royal Family's private chapel, the State Dining Room, the Crimson Drawing Room and various ancillary rooms on adjacent floors. By good fortune the rooms worst affected by the fire were empty at the time, since they were being rewired. Restoration of the fire-damaged areas was completed five years later on 20 November 1997, the Golden Wedding Anniversary of HM The Queen and HRH The Duke of Edinburgh, and is inscribed on a tablet in the reredos of the former chapel.

A yellow Lamborghini Miura SV (built in 1972) foregrounded beneath the iconic Round Tower.
© Doug Harding.

A 1918 Straker-Squire X2/prototype with a 'zebra style' paint pattern. The 4 litre 6-cylinder engine inside this Brooklands racer was capable of around 110 mph.
© Doug Harding.

St George's Hall is one of the most magnificent and historic rooms in the castle and has for six centuries been associated with the Order of the Garter.[22] The imposing 55 metre room can accommodate up to 160 guests for formal dinners and official state banquets. The original romantic

Gothic interior was inspired by Sir Walter Scott, whose novels were greatly admired by King George IV. During the 1992 fire the ceiling and the east wall were entirely destroyed. The new hammer-beam roof is constructed entirely of green oak, using medieval carpentry techniques, and is the largest timber roof built in the twentieth century. On the ceiling there are over 1000 shields of Garter Knights and a number of blank shields, which represent 'degraded' Knights, expelled from the Order at different times.[23] One of the most impressive Semi-State rooms is the Crimson Drawing Room, with a large bay window that overlooks the Eastern Terrace. It is only open at certain times of the year, because it is used regularly by the Royal Family. The tour of the State Apartments eventually leads you out into a courtyard, under the shadow of the Round Tower, near the railings that enclose The Quadrangle.

By kind permission of the Dean and Canons of Windsor. Low-angle shot of St George's Chapel, with its three polygonal chantry chapels, as seen from King Henry VIII Gate. Chantry chapels were originally set up both as burial places and as chantries where masses could be said daily for the souls of the departed. It was believed that such masses would speed the soul through purgatory towards eternal rest in Heaven. © *Doug Harding.*

Aerial view of St George's Chapel and the Horseshoe Cloister. © *Jason Hawkes.*

The Lower Ward and St George's Chapel

St George's Chapel dominates the Lower Ward of Windsor Castle and is one of the finest examples of the Perpendicular style of late gothic architecture.[24] For over 500 years it has been home to the College of St George and the Order of the Garter. Visiting in 1910, the poet Edward Thomas described it as: *'exquisite and elaborate. It holds and embalms the sunlight'.*[25] Within the chapel are the tombs of 10 royal monarchs, including King Henry VIII, King Charles I and King George VI.

There has been a chapel here since the reign of King Henry III on the site of the current Albert Memorial Chapel,[26] and traces of the original chapel still remain: the six Purbeck columns, the arches of the narthex now forming the vestibule, and the exquisite door of wrought iron scroll-work, once covered with scarlet gesso, and still bearing the signature of the smith, Gilebertus.[27] A significant moment in the history of St George's Chapel occurred in November 1312 when a prince was born to King Edward II and Queen Isabella. According to Ashmole,[28] the prince was born in auspicious circumstances: *'the 6 degree of the sign Scorpio ascending, and the 18 degree of Leo culminating'*. His horoscope is still to be seen in an Elizabethan painted glass window in St George's Chapel.[29] It was a fortunate day indeed because the prince, who would later become King Edward III, besides carrying out extensive building projects, also founded the Order of the Garter, with Windsor as its temporal and spiritual home. Inspired by tales of King Arthur and the chivalry of his knights, he decided to hold a Round Table at Windsor in 1343. He issued invitations not only to English knights, but also to three hundred foreign knights, to participate in jousts and festivities. The tournament was undoubtedly a success, because the king repeated it in 1345 and commanded a circular building to be constructed in the Upper Bailey to house his Round Table. Soon afterwards his attention was diverted to foreign affairs at Crécy, northern France, where

By kind permission of the Dean and Canons of Windsor. The original Tudor stone royal beasts placed on the pinnacles of the Chapel were deemed unsafe by Sir Christopher Wren and removed in 1682. They were replaced in the 1920s, when it was realised that their combined weight was architecturally important in holding the whole structure together. Many of the beasts now hold weather vanes, which also act as lightning conductors. © *Doug Harding*.

he won a shattering victory in August 1346, with his son, the Black Prince, winning his spurs leading the van.[30] On their return the King and Prince celebrated their victories with a series of tournaments and established an order of knighthood based at Windsor containing his and the Black Prince's young companions. Thus King Edward III founded the Most Noble Order of the Garter as a society, fellowship and college of knights, consisting of the Sovereign and 25 Knights Companion, with the famous blue garter as a 'symbol of amity'. The Order represented the new ideals of chivalry and helped to diminish the dangers of political disaffection. Furthermore, the yearly feasts, the tournaments, and the opportunity of personal contact with the sovereign meant that that membership was soon regarded as the highest distinction.[31] King Edward III lost no time in establishing a religious background to this new institution and in August 1348 he founded the priestly college of St. George consisting of a Dean and 25 canons and in addition appointed 26 Poor Knights (now called Military Knights) to attend mass daily as substitutes for the Garter Knights, who would be accomplishing noble deeds elsewhere[32].

The next major re-structuring of the chapel occurred in the reign of King Edward IV who built the present St George's Chapel on a grand scale (perhaps to outdo his rival's chapel, then half-finished, across the Thames in Eton)[33]. It was a masterpiece of late Perpendicular architecture, divided in transepts half way down its length to accommodate an unusually long choir for the Knights of the Garter[34]. Building work continued in the reign of King Henry VII, who completed the roof with the magnificent fan vaulting seen today and rebuilt the framework of King Henry III and King Edward III's chapel to the east of it, intending to make it a shrine to the saintly King Henry VI (founder of Eton), but the process of canonisation never went through.[35] The chapel was completed in the reign of King Henry VIII (in 1528), with the magnificent fan vault over the crossing.

Looking east towards Windsor Castle from the A332 flyover. © *Doug Harding*.

Looking up at the Vicars' Hall and the Curfew Tower from Thames Street.

By kind permission of the Dean and Canons of Windsor. Each year on Garter Day, the Knights and Ladies of the Order gather in the State Apartments at the command of HM The Queen. New Knights and Ladies are invested with the insignia and mantle in the Garter Throne Room. After the investiture, the 24 members of the Order of the Garter process from the Upper Ward through the Castle precincts to St George's Chapel for the annual Garter Service.
© Doug Harding.

In addition to the daily services, the chapel is in regular use for ceremonial occasions, and the most celebrated of these is the service of the Most Noble Order of the Garter, which takes place in June, when the reigning monarch and the Knights and Ladies of the Order, attired in the robes of the Order, process with much pageantry, from the State Apartments in the Upper Ward, through the Norman Gate and the Lower Ward to the Great West Door of the Chapel for the annual service.[36] The Companions wear dark blue velvet robes adorned with the cross of St George surrounded by the Garter motto: 'Honi Soit Qui Mal Y Pense' (*Shame on him who thinks evil of it*). Their robes have a red velvet hood, worn on the right shoulder, and their hats are velvet bonnets with ostrich feathers.[37] Today the Order, which is Britain's highest order of chivalry, also includes members of the Royal Family and distinguished figures in the life of the nation.[38] The military connection to the Order is maintained by the Military Knights of Windsor, who are retired members of the armed services, and reside within the Lower Ward of the castle.

One of the visual highlights of the chapel is the Quire, with its pomp of

By kind permission of the Dean and Canons of Windsor. Highly ornamented organ pipes in the organ loft above the crossing. Each pipe is decorated with Garter badges, Tudor roses, greyhounds and dragons.

By kind permission of the Dean and Canons of Windsor. A pomp of banners hang beneath the magnificent fan-vaulted ceiling in the Quire of St George's Chapel. Above the stall of each living Companion of the Order of the Garter hangs his mantling, crest, helm, sword and banner. Many crests and coats of arms make use of visual or verbal puns. At the back of each oak stall is a stall plate, which remains in place after a Companion's death. There have been over 1000 Knights and Ladies of the Garter since the Order was founded in 1348, and nearly 800 stall plates remain in place.

banners, swords, helmets, mantels and arms of the Garter Knights. Since the early days of the Order, plates have been placed on the back of the stalls bearing the arms of the Knights. The plates are of copper or brass with gilded or silver surfaces on which the arms are either enamelled or painted.[39] In the centre of the Quire under a black ledger stone lies the tomb of King Henry VIII, Jane Seymour, King Charles I and a child of Queen Anne. John Evelyn visited in 1654 and *'saw the Castle and Chapel of St. George, where they have laid our blessed Martyr, King Charles, in the vault just before the altar'.*[40] The fan vaulting throughout the chapel is exquisite and in the North Choir Aisle, the design in which octagons fill the central spandrels between the fans, is unique to Windsor.[41]

Unlike most cathedrals, St George's Chapel is usually approached from the south where the buttresses are a prominent feature. The upper flying buttresses take much of the weight of the roof from the clerestory windows to the outer wall of the aisle.[42] The lower projecting buttresses increase in depth to the ground, with carvings of heraldic beasts placed on the pinnacles.

By kind permission of the Dean and Canons of Windsor. Heraldic beasts on the Chapel roof silhouetted against the lilac afterglow of a summer sunset. © *Doug Harding*.

By kind permission of the Dean and Canons of Windsor. A service of choral Evensong in the Quire with Lay Clerks and Choristers in attendance. The Chapel Choir sings regularly at around eight services a week during term time, and is made up of Lay Clerks (professional male singers) and boy Choristers (between the ages of 8 and 13). All services are open to the public, who can experience the sublime singing of a choral Evensong and the flawless acoustics of the Quire, from their seat in the Garter Stalls. © *Doug Harding.*

The present day College of St George, is a community of people who live and work together to offer worship to God, prayers for the Sovereign and the Order of the Garter, service to society and hospitality to visitors. It consists of St George's School, St George's House, the Military Knights of Windsor, the Chapter Library & Archives and the Choir as well as St George's Chapel itself.[43] The buildings owned and occupied by the College, take up a quarter of Windsor Castle together with the school buildings outside the north wall. The Chapel Choir sings regularly at about eight services a week, during term time, and consists of up to 23 boy Choristers (between the ages of 8 and 13) and 12

By kind permission of the Dean and Canons of Windsor. A wide-angle view of The Great West Door of St George's Chapel from the lawn of the Horseshoe Cloister. © *Doug Harding.*

Lay Clerks providing the adult voices of alto, tenor and bass.[44] The boys are educated at St George's School, which is situated in the Castle grounds; the Lay Clerks (male professional singers) reside in the Horseshoe Cloister and on Denton's Commons. The primary function of the Chapel Choir is to sing the daily services, the Opus Dei, and the large repertoire of music drawn from all ages and traditions. The chorister boys have been members of the College by statute since its foundation and a detailed study has been made of their role in chapel life from medieval times to the 1970s.[45]

By kind permission of the Dean and Canons of Windsor. A soft-focus portrait of St George's Chapel enveloped in December snow, as viewed from the Military Knights' Lodgings. © *Doug Harding.*

St George's Chapel and College buildings are not, as many people think, either the property or financial responsibility of the State, the Church of England or the Royal Family. The College relies almost entirely on visitor admission charges for the routine maintenance of the Chapel. However, these cannot fully meet the costs of maintaining and running the Chapel. The Friends of St George's & Descendants of the Knights of the Garter are a network of individuals who support St George's on a regular basis.[46] Founded in 1931, The Friends offer financial support to the Dean and Canons of Windsor on whom the sole responsibility of maintaining St George's Chapel, its Cloisters and medieval lodgings lies. They are also part of a wider community of over 4000 members worldwide, committed to the values espoused by the College of St George and keen to preserve its magnificent buildings for future generations. Many of them also volunteer their services to St George's in various ways: from assisting in the Chapel shop to stewarding visitors; from helping to keep the Chapel clean to raising funds. A more detailed account of St George's Chapel may be found in the official publications.[47, 48, 49]

A view from a high balcony on the High Street, looking towards Queen Victoria's Statue and the Salisbury Tower. © *Doug Harding.*

By kind permission of the Dean and Canons of Windsor. Detail of heraldic beasts on the roof of St George's Chapel, looking east towards the Round Tower. © *Doug Harding.*

In recent times St George's Chapel has played host to a number of Royal marriages: the service of prayer and dedication following the marriage of HRH The Prince of Wales and HRH The Duchess of Cornwall on 9 April 2005, the marriage of HRH Prince Henry of Wales and Ms. Meghan Markle on 19 May 2018 and the marriage of HRH Princess Eugenie of York and Mr Jack Brooksbank on 12 October 2018.

In the far right-hand corner of the Lower Ward is a small gateway leading to the Horseshoe Cloister, a row of timber-framed buildings with herringboned brickwork, originally built by King Edward IV in ca.1480 for the priest-vicars of St George's Chapel.[50] The outline of the cloister is said to represent the shape of a fetterlock, one of King Edward IV's badges.[51] A sympathetic restoration of the cloister was performed in the 1870s by Sir Giles Gilbert Scott. The houses now provide lodgings for the lay clerks (men singers of the Chapel Choir) and the virger.

By kind permission of the Dean and Canons of Windsor. HRH Prince Harry and Ms. Meghan Markle (The Duke and Duchess of Sussex) leave Windsor Castle in an open-topped landau after their marriage in St George's Chapel on 19 May 2018. The couple journeyed around the streets of Windsor, cheered along by flag-waving crowds, before returning to the Castle via the Long Walk for the lunchtime reception at St George's Hall. It is estimated that a UK audience of around 18 million tuned in to watch the live broadcast of the Royal Wedding from St George's Chapel.
© Doug Harding.

Beyond the far corner of the cloister lies the Curfew Tower, containing the eight bells of the Chapel, which are chimed every three hours through a clock mechanism dating from the seventeenth century.[52] The sharply-pointed conical roof of the tower was added later around 1863 and the picturesque houses which had encroached on the castle ditch were swept away.[53] The exterior of the castle was thus *'shaken more free of the little town clambering and clustering about it'*.[54] The impressive gateway to the castle, where the visitor tour ends, is known as King Henry VIII Gate, built in 1511, when the castle was already over 400 years old.[55]

A view of the Curfew Tower from the High Street.

Windsor Castle Guards, in their instantly recognisable scarlet tunics and bearskin caps, stand around the entrance to King Henry VIII Gate.

Changing the Guard

The ceremony of Changing the Guard (also known as Guard Mount) is one of the visual highlights of a visit to Windsor and takes place in the castle precincts (usually the Lower Ward) with the New and Old Guard entering and leaving through King Henry VIII Gate. When the Sovereign is in official residence the ceremony occurs on the lawn of the Quadrangle, outside the Royal Apartments, with the New Guard marching to the top of Castle Hill and entering through St George's Gate.

Irish Guard on sentry duty in the Lower Ward, enjoying some peace and quiet before the visitors arrive.
© *Doug Harding.*

Grenadier Guards file past Queen Victoria's Statue as they return to barracks after Guard Mount.

The ceremony begins with the New Guard and Regimental Band assembling outside the Guard Room at Victoria Barracks, from whence they depart at 10:45 am to march up Sheet Street, wheeling left into the High Street, past the Parish Church and the Guildhall, before bearing right onto Castle Hill by Queen Victoria's Statue and up the hill into Windsor Castle. The New Guard remains on duty for 24 or 48 hours, consisting of 2 hours sentry duty followed by a 4 hour break. Following the Guard Mount the Old Guard and Band parade along the High Street on their way back to barracks.

The band of the Welsh Guards parade along the High Street on their way back to the Victoria Barracks in Sheet Street.

The Windsor Castle Guard is provided by one of five Regiments of Foot Guards, of the Household Division, in their full-dress uniform of scarlet tunics and bearskin caps, accompanied by a Regimental Band and Corps of Drums.[56] These are: the Grenadier Guards, the Coldstream Guards, the Scots Guards, the Irish Guards and the Welsh Guards. The scarlet uniforms and bearskin caps of the troops may appear the same, at first glance, but there are subtle differences.[57] For example, the button spacing and shoulder badge on each regiment's tunic is different: the Grenadier Guards have single button spacing and a royal cipher, the Scots Guards have three button spacing and a thistle star. Recruits to the Guards Regiments go through a thirty week gruelling training programme at the Infantry Training Centre, which is two weeks longer than the training for the regular line infantry regiments of the British Army.

The Coldstream Guards march up the High Street towards the Guildhall for the ceremony of Changing the Guard. The red plume on the right hand side of the bearskin identifies the regiment.

The band of the Household Calvary parade past Queen Victoria's Statue as they return to barracks.

The band of the Coldstream Guards parade up the High Street, dressed in their winter uniform of long grey coats.

CHAPTER 2
WINDSOR TOWN

Residents of Windsor are justifiably proud of their town and for good reason: it is, after all, one of the most popular tourist destinations in the United Kingdom and indeed the world.[1] Just 10 miles from Heathrow Airport and around 25 miles from the centre of London, the town is readily accessible by car, coach and rail. Although the Castle, and its historic treasures are the big draw, there is a great deal more to discover, experience and enjoy in the town itself. Remarkable monuments and stunning structures, steeped in history, are around every corner and some of the town's highlights are described below.

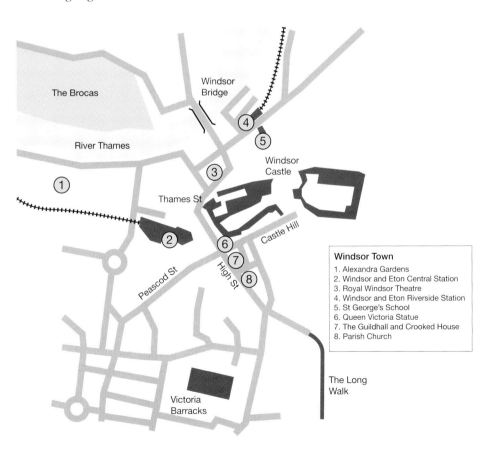

Windsor Town
1. Alexandra Gardens
2. Windsor and Eton Central Station
3. Royal Windsor Theatre
4. Windsor and Eton Riverside Station
5. St George's School
6. Queen Victoria Statue
7. The Guildhall and Crooked House
8. Parish Church

View of the Castle from the ferris wheel installed in Alexandra Gardens (ca. 2010). © *Doug Harding.*
Below: Aerial view of Windsor town from high above the Brocas. © *Doug Harding.*

Colourful banners, interspersed with Union Jacks, promote The Royal Windsor Horse Show 2015. The grade I listed Guildhall stands tall amidst the pageantry. During the First World War it was used as a recruiting station, and now houses The Windsor and Royal Borough Museum on the ground floor.

The Queen Victoria Statue

At the foot of Castle Hill there is a bronze statue of Queen Victoria, which was commissioned and constructed for the Queen's Golden Jubilee celebrations. It was paid for by public subscription and unveiled on 22 June 1887, with the Queen herself in attendance.[2] The sculptor was Sir Joseph Edgar Boehm, who designed and erected the statue on a red Aberdeen granite base. The statue depicts the Queen holding an orb and sceptre and wearing her miniature state crown,[3] which she wore over her widow's cap. The sceptre is an ornamental staff carried by a monarch on ceremonial occasions to signify authority and sovereignty. The orb, topped with a crucifix, symbolizes Christ's dominion over the world. In 1897, a canopy made of wood and canvas was temporarily erected around the statue for Queen Victoria's Diamond Jubilee celebrations. A little over three years later, the Queen's coffin was brought to Windsor and laid to rest at the Frogmore mausoleum, alongside her beloved husband, Prince Albert.[4]

Bronze statue of Queen Victoria erected in 1887 to commemorate her Golden Jubilee. The monarch's reign continued for over sixty-three years, until her death in 1901. She was interred at Frogmore Mausoleum with her beloved Albert, the Prince Consort, who pre-deceased her by forty years. Behind the statue, under a dark and foreboding sky, the Garter Tower stands sentinel.

Just across the road from the statue is the Harte and Garter Hotel – one of the most historic hotels in Windsor. It is an amalgamation of two fourteenth century inns: The Garter Inn, named after the Most Noble Order of the Garter, and The White Harte, named in honour of the Royal Emblem worn by King Richard II.[5] The Garter Inn was one of the settings for Shakespeare's *'The Merry Wives of Windsor'*.

If you bear left along the High Street you will come to the Glorious Britain shop. In the doorway there is a circular white plaque to commemorate H.G. Wells, who worked here in 1880, for Rodgers and Denyer, as a drapers' assistant. Wells is best known for his work in the science fiction genre and notable works include: *'The War of the Worlds'*, *'The Time Machine'* and *'The Invisible Man'*.

Queen Victoria statue set against the backdrop of the 'The Harte and Garter Hotel'. Photographs from 1961 indicate that the hotel, which was built in the nineteenth century, was originally called 'The White Hart', as indicated by the stone fascia under the roof.

The Guildhall

The Guildhall, sited on Windsor High Street, close to the Castle, is an elegant seventeenth century building, which is also home to the Windsor and Royal Borough Museum. The building (which should more accurately be called 'The Town Hall') was designed by Sir Thomas Fitz, and its foundation stone was laid on 5th September 1687.[6] Sir Thomas died before the project could be completed and Sir Christopher Wren continued his work and made it ready for occupation on 17 October 1689. The design of the building allowed for a corn market beneath the meeting chamber above. One curious fact about the structure is that the four Portland Stone pillars in the centre of the corn market do not actually support the ceiling. The council were concerned that the floor of the chamber might collapse if left unsupported, although the architect (Sir Christopher Wren) was adamant that additional support was not required. To prove a point, he complied with their request for additional columns, but left them just short of the ceiling.[7]

The traffic flows freely again past the Guildhall and along Windsor High Street, as the crowds disperse after the guard change.

The band of the Welsh Guards (returning to barracks) march past the Guildhall after the guard change on Castle Hill. The regiment may be identified by the emblem on the collar (a leek) and the button spacing on the uniform (groups of 5).

Nowadays, the Guildhall is one of the most popular wedding ceremony venues in the Borough and has two rooms available for hire[8]: an imposing Council Chamber (seating 100 people), which houses a fine collection of royal portraits spanning the years between Queen Elizabeth I and HM Queen Elizabeth II; and the more intimate Ascot Room (seating 15 people) – the venue chosen by HRH Prince Charles for his civil ceremony in April 2005, and later the same year by Sir Elton John for his civil partnership.

The statue in the niche on the north side of the building is that of Queen Anne, and was installed by the Corporation of Windsor in 1707. The companion statue on the south side is her royal consort, Prince George of Denmark, dressed in a Roman military habit. Underneath, in the frieze of the entablature, there are Latin inscriptions which describe each statue.

Next door to the Guildhall is the famous Crooked House - one of the most photographed buildings in Windsor. It is sighted on the corner of the High Street and Queen Charlotte Street – a tiny cobblestone passageway, less than 52 feet in length, and the shortest street in the country.[9] The seventeenth century oak-framed building suffers from a distinctive lean.

The Crooked House, one of the most photographed buildings in Windsor, with a bevy of pink flowers in the foreground.

The gravity-defying Crooked House, when the premises were used as a tea room (ca.2011).

There seems to be two conflicting theories about the perilous lean: one that it was built using poorly chosen, unseasoned oak and shortly after construction began to warp into a distinctly crooked appearance, which has become it's defining feature; the other that the lean only appeared after adjoining buildings were demolished in the late 1820s. There are also unconfirmed reports of a tunnel which ran from the basement of the Crooked House into Windsor Castle and was used by King Charles II and Nell Gwynn for secret trysts.[10].

Looking down Queen Charlotte Street at twilight towards 'The Carpenters Arms'.

Windsor Parish Church

The present church building dates from 1822 when it replaced an earlier structure with Saxon arches and Norman work that was in dire need of expensive renovation.[11] The outer walls follow the plan of the medieval church, with old burial vaults lying beneath the present floor. The architect, Charles Hollis, designed the building with cast iron columns and ribs and it was consecrated by the Bishop of Salisbury on 22 June, 1822. The eight bells, were transferred from the earlier building, and are rung for royal occasions, at the Sovereign's expense. Around the outside walls of the church there

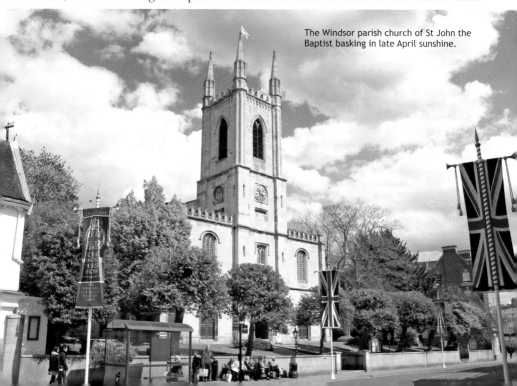

The Windsor parish church of St John the Baptist basking in late April sunshine.

are several war memorials that were retained from the previous church, as well as more recent commemorative plaques. The hatchment of Richard Gallis, host of the Garter Inn (died 1580), is one of the local personalities that Shakespeare may have drawn upon for his *'Merry Wives of Windsor'*. Near the main altar there is a memorial to Sir Sidney Camm, designer of the Hawker Hurricane and other RAF aircraft. The Royal Pew was a gift from Princess Augusta (daughter of King George III) who regularly worshipped in the parish church. It is fronted

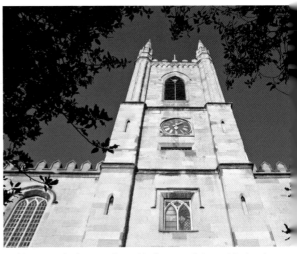

Looking up at the honey-coloured bell tower of the parish church.

by wooden panels carved by Grinling Gibbons, each showing a pelican feeding its young (look out for the peapod - Gibbons' signature); the wooden panels were formally part of the altar rail in St George's Chapel, Windsor. The painting of 'The Last Supper' by Franz de Cleyn, court painter to James I, hangs on the west wall, and was given to the parish church by King George III.

The stained glass window on the north aisle illustrates the words in Luke's Gospel (Luke 10:42) to Martha and Mary, that contemplation is better than anxious servitude.

Windsor and Eton Stations

Windsor and Eton Central Station[12] is the terminus point for a branch line that connects Windsor to the neighbouring Borough of Slough. It was opened on 8 October 1849, but only after considerable opposition from the leadership at Eton College, who were convinced that the proximity of a railway might lead the Eton boys astray.[13] The station entrance is situated on Thames Street close to Castle Hill. The original building was completely rebuilt by the Great Western Railway (GWR) in 1897 to mark Queen Victoria's Diamond Jubilee, with a much grander frontage and an interior reminiscent of Paddington. Two island platforms and a bay on the south side were provided. Most of the original station building has now been converted into a tourist-orientated shopping centre (Windsor Royal Shopping Centre).

The station is approached via a 1.9 km brick viaduct and Windsor Railway Bridge[14] – a wrought iron 'bow and string' structure, designed by Isambard Kingdom Brunel. The single-span design comprises three bowstring trusses, which created two bays for the original GWR tracks. The bridge carries the branch line over the River Thames on the reach between Romney Lock and Boveney Lock.

A train passes over the brick-built viaduct on the Eton side of the river – part of the GWR branch line from Windsor to Slough.

A full-size replica steam locomotive (GWR Achilles Class 4-2-2) named *The Queen* is incorporated as a feature of a restaurant on the station concourse. The original was built at the Swindon Works in 1894 and named *Emlyn* after Lord Emlyn, Chairman of the GWR company. In 1897, the locomotive was repainted in GWR livery and renamed *The Queen* to pull the six new carriages of the Royal Train.[15]

Close to the river, on the Datchet Road, there is a second station serving Windsor, named (appropriately) Windsor and Eton Riverside. This is a terminus point for direct services between Windsor and Waterloo and is operated by South Western Railway. The route stops at several key stations, including Staines, Richmond and Clapham Junction. The line was opened as far as Datchet in August 1848, but extension of the line to Windsor was delayed until December 1849.[16] The wall on the Datchet Road side of the station contains a long series of arches (parallel to the platform) which link the station concourse to the former Royal Waiting Room, built for Queen Victoria.

The coat of arms on the front of a full-size replica steam locomotive *The Queen*, incorporated as a feature on the central station concourse.

A GWR train passes over the viaduct with the honey-coloured pinnacles of Eton College Chapel in the background.

In 2009, an ambitious scheme was proposed by a local businessman to connect the Great Western and South Western Railway lines in Windsor with a tunnel and a new single station. The new line – The Windsor Link Railway (WLR)[17] – would be entirely privately funded, to the tune of £370 million. The scheme would create a link between Staines and Slough and thereby increase service frequency to and from London. Improvements to the Windsor riverside, catalysed by the infrastructure, would include a park extended by 33% and reconnected with the river, 1,600 additional car parking spaces, new homes for local people and more community facilities. Plans for Britain's first self-funded rail link, for over 100 years, were submitted by WLR and its investment consortium to the Department of Transport in July 2018 and, if the scheme is approved, the promotors predict that the first trains could be running on the new line by 2024.

The Windsor and Eton Riverside Station – a terminus point for trains operated by South Western Railway. The station stands opposite 'The Royal Windsor pub' and the entrance to St George's School, Windsor Castle.

The Theatre Royal

'We are all in the gutter, but some of us are looking at the stars'

Oscar Wilde, Lady Windermere's Fan

This splendid theatre nestles in the shadow of the castle and is the only unsubsidised producing theatre in Britain to operate all year round.[18] The repertoire is wide, ranging from the classics and traditional pantomime to first productions of new work, some of which are subsequently transferred to the West End. The Theatre Royal has gained a reputation for the quality of its productions and is currently one of Britain's leading theatres.

The entrance to the Theatre Royal, with the newly erected security barriers nearby. There have been complaints about the barriers, but the need to protect the public against potential acts of terror, whilst maintaining civil liberties, remains a constant balancing act.

In 1793 a theatre was built on the Windsor High Street and the opening production was a farce called 'Everyone has his faults'. King George III frequently attended the theatre when in residence at the castle, and one side of the lower tier of boxes was reserved for him and his entourage. During this time, the Windsor theatre was not open all the year round, but only for the six weeks in the summer when Eton College was closed for holidays. It was perhaps felt that the theatre might have a corrupting influence on the boys. In 1815, the citizens of Windsor raised the £6,000 needed to build a new theatre on the site of the present building, which was gutted by fire in 1908. The theatre was rebuilt and opened in December 1910. In 1938 a repertory company was established and some weeks later King George VI and Queen Elizabeth attended a performance of *'The Rose without a thorn'*; the next morning the theatre was headline news. This set a precedent which has been followed by the present Queen and other members of the Royal Family. In 1988 the company celebrated its fiftieth birthday, an occasion graced by the presence of Her Majesty Queen Elizabeth, the Queen Mother.

Alexandra Gardens

Plans to create a riverside garden on the banks of the Thames date from 1893, but it took another nineteen years for the gardens to be sufficiently complete to permit the planting of a London Plane, in August 1902, to celebrate the Coronation of Edward VII and his Queen, Alexandra.[19]

A bandstand was also erected on the site and the band of the Royal Horse Guards played there regularly. In 2016, a replacement bandstand was built to celebrate the unique and long-standing links between HM The Queen, the Armed Forces and Windsor. It also commemorated Queen Elizabeth II as the longest-reigning monarch in British history and, in turn, the longest-reigning Head of the Armed Forces. The role of the armed forces is explored in the six commemorative plaques on the bandstand; each of the plaques displays one important event involving the armed forces from each of the six decades of The Queen's reign.

The bandstand in Alexandra Gardens, basking in early spring sunshine.

If plans for the Windsor Link Railway are approved, then Alexandra Gardens is on course for a make-over in the next few years. It will be re-landscaped and enlarged by 33%, reconnected with the Thames and edged with a new Georgian-style terrace[20].

This full-size replica of a Battle of Britain fighter aircraft was unveiled on the Thames promenade (near Alexandra Gardens) in July 2012. The Hawker Hurricane was designed by Sir Sydney Camm, renowned throughout the world as the 'Brunel of aero engineers'. Born in Alma Road, Windsor, the son of a carpenter's apprentice, he was educated at the Royal Free School in Bachelor's Acre. Without any formal engineering training, he rose to become one of the world's greatest aeronautical engineers, with 50 designs to his credit and over 26,000 aircraft built.

This ornamental fountain, inspired by the crown jewels, was created in The Goswells to mark the Queen's Diamond Jubilee in 2012. The water feature comprises a long canal, with a line of dramatic vertical jets, and a circular pool at the centre. In the middle of the pool is a geyser with a "crown" of 60 water jets. © *Doug Harding.*

St George's School, Windsor Castle

Originally founded in 1348 to educate the choristers of St George's Chapel, the school has developed into a vibrant and successful Prep School of some 350 children, aged from three to thirteen.[21]

The current building, erected in 1802, was originally called Travers' College, and used to accommodate the Naval Knights of Windsor (part of the Military Knights). Due to their disreputable behaviour and irregular attendance at Chapel services, the First Lord of the Admiralty regretfully recommended their dissolution. They were finally disbanded, but not without protest, under the 'Naval Knights of Windsor (dissolution) Act 1892.[22]

Since the building was now vacant, Canon Dalton suggested that it might be used as a choir school for St George's Chapel choristers. After much negotiation, the Admiralty wrote to the Chapter Clerk, Richard Cope, on 5 October 1892, consenting to a 42 year lease of the building, at a reduced rent of £132 per annum[23].

Travers' College, once the home of the ill-fated Naval Knights, is now St George's School, Windsor Castle.

Aerial view of St George's School from the North Terrace of Windsor Castle

At a Chapter meeting on 2 August 1893 it was agreed that Travers' College should be renamed 'St George's School, Windsor Castle'. The new school opened on 21 September 1893, and was designed to provide for thirty boarders (twenty-four of whom were to be choristers) and ten day-boys[24]. The first headmaster Ashley Bickersteth, served only 18 months, but the next headmaster, H.F.W. Deane, succeeded in establishing a thoroughly efficient working pattern for the school. After his retirement in 1904, he maintained his connections with St George's Chapel and was elected librarian to the Chapter in 1906 and became assistant Chapter Clerk to Richard Cope in 1908.[25]

The majority of the children who now attend the school are day pupils, but the buildings are still home to around 23 choristers, who attend the school and live in the school's boarding house, rehearsing every morning and singing in St George's Chapel daily services, as well as on special occasions such as Garter Day and at Royal Weddings.

Tourism

Windsor is one of the major tourist attractions in South East England, and as such experiences very high levels of visitor activity. The lynchpin of the town's local economy is tourism, which supports one in ten jobs in the Borough. Windsor Castle is the largest and oldest inhabited castle in the world and high on the list of international tourist destinations. In the 2017/18 fiscal year it welcomed 1.44 million visitors,[26] which exceeded Buckingham Palace, during its summer opening (with just under half a million visitors). According to figures from the Royal Borough of Windsor and Maidenhead, 1.71 million visitor nights were spent in the district in 2017. Direct expenditure generated by tourism in Windsor & Maidenhead in 2017 was estimated to be around £423 million, and this tourism-related expenditure is estimated to have supported over 8,000 actual jobs (including part-time and seasonal employment) in Windsor & Maidenhead during 2017.[27] In such a tourist-driven economy, the effects of high visitor numbers on traffic congestion, local services and residents all require careful management.

An open-top double decker bus tour of Windsor and Eton is one way to explore the area and see the sights. The circular tour lasts approximately sixty minutes and offers multi-lingual commentary in 10 languages (including English)!

Relax and unwind as you experience the delights of the Long Walk and the Great Park from the comfort of an elegant horse-drawn carriage.

An outdoor souvenir stall at the entrance to Windsor Royal Shopping Centre, selling a variety of merchandise, celebrating all things English.

Wax-work replicas of two Coldstream Guards stand sentinel in McDonald's Windsor, circa 2010. The regiment may be identified by the emblem on the collar (a Garter Star) and the button spacing on the uniform (groups of 2).

CHAPTER 3

WINDSOR GREAT PARK

Windsor Great Park consists of 4800 acres of historic parkland, ancient woodland, forest trails and award-winning gardens to the south of Windsor Castle.[1] Less than 30 miles from central London, it provides local residents with a green haven for walking, cycling and horse riding.[2] Before the Norman Conquest in 1066, the Forest of Windsor (as it became known) was used by Saxon kings as a royal hunting forest. William the Conqueror continued this tradition, but went one step further by implementing Forest Law. This restricted the rights of the common man to use the forest and created a deer park which preserved the game for the King and his Court. Today the situation has turned full circle. The Great Park is managed by the Crown Estate and the public are now actively encouraged to visit and explore the parkland trails, the historical monuments and the horticultural displays.

White candle-like flowers of horse chestnut direct the eye towards King George IV gate, as tourists take a stroll up the Long Walk.

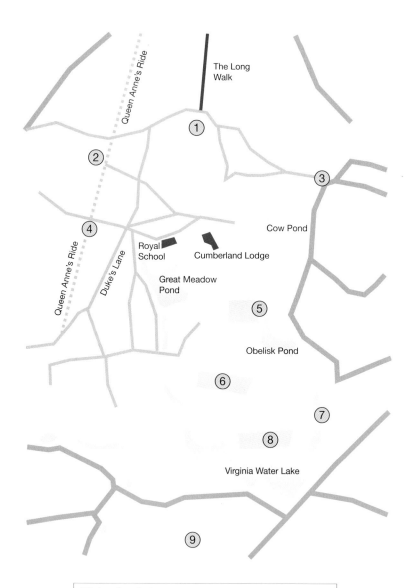

The Long Walk

Queen Anne's Ride

Cow Pond

Royal School

Cumberland Lodge

Great Meadow Pond

Queen Anne's Ride

Duke's Lane

Obelisk Pond

Virginia Water Lake

Windsor Great Park

1. The Copper Horse
2. The Village
3. Bishopsgate
4. Queen Elizabeth II Statue
5. The Savill Garden
6. Polo Grounds
7. Totem Pole
8. Valley Gardens
9. Fort Belvedere

Autumn leaves carpet the ground between the gilded avenues of chestnut and plane.

The Long Walk

After the Restoration of the Monarchy in 1660, when all lands seized by Parliament during the Civil War were reinstated, King Charles II began his restoration of the Great Park with gusto.[3] Perhaps inspired by the Great Canal at Versailles, he issued a warrant in 1680 for the creation of the Long Walk and spent much time and effort in acquiring the necessary land[4]. John Evelyn noted in his diary[5]: *'The King passed most of his time in hunting the stag, and walking in the park, which he was now planting with rows of trees'*. The planting of the avenue, with a double row of English elms (1652 trees), was completed by the time of his death in February 1685.[6] The elm trees flourished and reached a great size and a gravelled road was added in 1710 by Queen Anne to accommodate horse-drawn carriages. Two centuries later (in 1943), after a serious outbreak of elm disease, the trees were felled by hand, using a two man cross-cut saw.[7] The avenue was then replanted with an outer row of London planes and an inner row of horse chestnuts. The idea was to see which species fared best and then remove the weaker type.[8] As it turned out, both species survived, but the non-native horse chestnut is now showing some signs of stress.

Procession of landaus (convertible horse drawn carriages) setting out from Windsor Castle en route for Royal Ascot.

The Copper Horse — an equestrian statue of King George III on Snow Hill — marks the end of the Long Walk from Windsor Castle. The statue depicts the king as an emperor in the roman tradition, riding without stirrups, and was commissioned by his son King George IV.

The Copper Horse

At the end of The Long Walk, two and a half miles from Windsor Castle, there is an equestrian statue of King George III. The king is depicted as an emperor in roman tradition, riding without stirrups. It bears a striking resemblance to the equestrian statue of Marcus Aurelius on Capitoline Hill, Rome, which may have been its inspiration. There is a dedication in Latin, on the rocky plinth, which reads: *'Georgio Tertio Patri Optimo Georgius Rex' (George III best of fathers King George IV).*[9] Historians have pondered what this might mean, since Hanoverian kings were notorious for having bad relations with their heirs. Perhaps it was a final act of contrition of a dying king towards an estranged father (King George IV died a year before the statue was erected on Snow Hill). It is certainly the most striking monument in the Great Park – an icon visible for miles of unrivalled grandeur, in direct line of sight of Windsor Castle.

View of Windsor Castle and The Long Walk from Snow Hill.

During his reign, King George III acquired the sobriquet 'Farmer George, the Squire of Windsor' due to his simple domestic life, his paternalistic role as the nation's father and his zeal for the theory and practice of agriculture[10]. Unlike his father, George IV led a dissolute life in his youth, describing himself as *'rather too fond of women and wine'*. In November 1810, when King George III became too mentally ill to rule,[11] his son became Regent, under the terms of the Regency Act (1811). He ascended the throne as King George IV in 1820 and his character was in part redeemed by his linguistic and intellectual abilities, and his astute judgement of the arts.[12] He patronized Wyatville's restoration of Windsor Castle and the architect John Nash, who developed Regent Street and Regent's Park. His most famous architectural triumph was the exotic Royal Pavilion at Brighton.

The Copper Horse was the work of Richard Westmacott, who revived large-scale bronze casting in Britain[13] and is made of brass (not copper). To construct the statue, 25 tons of brass canons were melted down in the foundry at Pimlico. Due to its sheer size it was cast in sections and then conveyed to Windsor for reassembly. One horse leg was damaged in transit and had to be recast. Sir Jeffry Wyatville was responsible for the plinth, which was made of brickwork and faced with granite. The sculpture was finally erected on Snow Hill in October 1831, and is still a commanding presence and focus of attention almost 200 years later.

Two outriders on Windsor Greys lead the procession of landaus as they pass the end of the Long Walk near Snow Hill.

Warm orange light reveals footprints in the snow, as visitors take the Long Walk home on a cold February afternoon.

On 19 May 2012 a spectacular flypast of 78 aircraft took place over the Copper Horse, as part of the Queen's Diamond Jubilee celebrations. Nine Typhoon fighter jets opened the event, followed by a large mixed formation, which included helicopters, a Lancaster and Spitfires from the Battle of Britain Memorial Flight, Tucanos (forming the number '60') and Hawks (forming 'E II R'). Closing the event were the world-famous Red Arrows, in a Diamond Nine formation, trailing red, white and blue smoke above the Long Walk and over the skies of Windsor.

Royal Ascot

Each year Ascot Racecourse holds a special programme of events in June, attended by HM The Queen and members of The Royal Family. The event (Royal Ascot) has become Britain's most popular race meeting, anticipated and revered the world over, attracting around 300,000 visitors over the five day period.[14] HM The Queen, who has had an interest in horses since childhood, is owner and breeder of many thoroughbred horses – some of which have won races at Royal Ascot. The Racecourse was originally founded by Queen Anne in 1711, and since its foundation has received Royal patronage from a further eleven monarchs.

HM The Queen and HRH Prince Philip travelling through Windsor Great Park to Royal Ascot, in June 2010. Each year HM The Queen and her guests leave Windsor Castle by royal car and transfer to the famous landaus at Duke's Lane to arrive at Ascot racecourse in the finest possible style.

Each day of Royal Ascot, a procession of landaus (convertible horse drawn carriages) set out from Windsor Castle, around midday, along the Long Walk and pass the Copper Horse thirty minutes later. Following the two outriders, there are four carriages, each pulled by four horses - either Windsor Greys or Cleveland Bays.[15] The Greys – standing at least 16.1 hands (1.65 m) at the withers – are chosen for their stamina and steady temperament[16]. The Semi-state landaus, used for the occasion, are postilion-driven and suspended on elliptical springs. The low shell construction makes for maximum visibility of the occupants in their Ascot attire.

The Duke and Duchess of Cambridge looking through the window of a Royal Ascot landau, in June 2016, at the change-over point in Duke's Lane .

HM The Queen and her guests leave Windsor Castle just after lunch in State cars (usually Rolls-Royce Phantom VIs) and transfer to the famous landaus at Duke's Lane (known as 'the Change') around 1.40 pm. Members of the public are allowed to watch the Royal Party transfer to the carriages, before they continue their journey through the Great Park towards Ascot Racecourse.

HM The Queen, en route for Royal Ascot 2011, wearing the famous Williamson Jonquil brooch. The central gemstone (of 23.6 carats) is said to be the finest pink diamond in existence, and was given to Princess Elizabeth in 1947 as a wedding present.

Queen Anne's Ride

Windsor Castle was Queen Anne's favourite summer residence[17] and despite her dropsy and stoutness, she was addicted to the chase. Driving a narrow, one-seated chaise with high wheels, she enjoyed following the hunt through the forest. The ride itself was laid out in 1708 by Henry Wise[18] to allow Queen Anne quick access to the Forest to indulge her passion for hunting. It was originally planted with elm and lime, but the trees did not fare well and replanting was necessary in 1813[19]. The trees were eventually felled in 1993 and replanted with 1000 oaks to commemorate 1000 years of the office of High Sheriff. The first tree was planted by the Park Ranger, HRH Prince Philip, Duke of Edinburgh. The millstone statue which celebrates the replanting has a circular hole in the centre through which you can view Windsor Castle, three miles away. Further along Queen Anne's Ride is an equestrian statue of HM Queen Elizabeth II, by Philip Jackson, commissioned to mark the Golden Jubilee in 2002. The mistletoed limes surrounding the statue are the oldest survivors of the original planting. The ride continues south, past this point, into the Deerpen and terminates close to Prince Consort's Gate.[20]

Snow-covered equestrian statue of Queen Elizabeth II silhouetted against an October sunset. © *Kevin Bishop.*

The millstone statue, which celebrates the replanting of 1000 oaks on Queen Anne's Ride, has a circular hole in the centre, through which Windsor Castle can be seen, 3 miles away.

The Village

It may come as a surprise to find an entire village community existing within the bounds of Windsor Great Park.[21] The Village was originally built in the centre of the Great Park in the 1930s to provide homes for Royal Estate workers, and the communal hub is now shared equally between the 'Village Shop' and the 'York Club'. The latter is a members-only club for residents and employees of the Crown Estate, but it can be hired out for private functions. The business end of the village is centred on the Prince Consort's Workshops and the Crown Estate Office (both of which are out of bounds to visitors, unless on Estate business).

Other notable buildings in this section of the Park include: The Royal School and Cumberland Lodge. The latter now functions as a charity that empowers people, through dialogue and debate, to promote progress towards more peaceful, open and inclusive societies.[22]

Polo and Smith's Lawn

Probably the most famous polo club in the world (Guards Polo Club) is situated in the heart of Windsor Great Park on Smith's Lawn. The club was founded in 1955 by HRH The Duke of Edinburgh, who remains the Club President to this day,[23] and retains a keen interest in all activities of the club. Guards Polo Club is host to more than 500 matches a season, making it the largest club in Europe. Some of the sport's most prestigious tournaments are played here, including the world-class Cartier Queen's Cup, and the Royal Windsor Cup.[24] There is also a Royal Box which is in regular use by HM The Queen and members of the Royal Family. It is decorated and arranged to meet the highest standards, and offers some of the finest corporate hospitality available, allowing guests to enjoy the polo in style.

The Cartier Queen's Cup polo match in progress on Smith's Lawn in 2009. © *Doug Harding.*

Polo is a one of the oldest team games played on horseback[25] and the objective is to score goals against the opposition, by driving a small white ball into the opponent's goal, using a long-handled wooden mallet. Each polo team consists of four riders and their ponies. The match is divided into chukkas, each lasting seven minutes, with an interval of 3 minutes between each one. The playing field (approximately six soccer fields in area) is carefully maintained, with closely mowed turf providing a fast, safe playing surface. At half-time, spectators are invited onto the field to

The Band of the Irish Guards at the Guards Polo Club, Windsor Great Park.

participate in a polo tradition called "divot stamping" – to replace the mounds of earth torn up by the ponies' hooves during the match.

Polo ponies tend to be swift and agile so they can turn and follow the ball through its many movements. During competition, the ponies have their tails docked and the skirt of the tail braided and folded up against the tailbone.[26] It is typical for a player to have numerous horses available for each match, using a separate horse for each chukka. Various breeds of polo ponies are used in the game, but in recent years crosses of Thoroughbreds and Criollo horses from Argentina have become popular. The public are allowed to watch the polo for free on Smith's Lawn, provided they remain behind the designated barriers.

A polo match in progress on Smith's Lawn. During half-time, spectators are invited to replace the divots torn up by the horses' hooves. © *Doug Harding*.

Smith's Lawn has also a short history as an airfield. It was set up in the 1920s and used by the Prince of Wales (later Edward VIII) as his own private grass airfield.[27] In WWII it became the dispersal point for a variety of smaller aircraft, with two Vickers-Armstrongs factories set up close by, after a major Luftwaffe attack on their main base in Brooklands. HRH The Duke of Edinburgh took off from Smith's Lawn in a de Havilland Chipmunk in December 1952, on his first solo flight, and was the last person to officially fly from the airfield early in 1953. In 2006, a memorial was unveiled on the site of the disused airfield by The Duke of Edinburgh.[28]

Copper Beech tree on the edge of the polo grounds, Smith's Lawn.

Virginia Water Lake

On his return from Holland in 1747, the Duke of Cumberland (the youngest son of King George II) sought employment for his demobilised soldiers, by carrying out extensive alterations in the Great Park.[29] He was assisted by Thomas Sandby, as Deputy Ranger, who was joined soon after by his artist brother Paul, whose series of watercolours (mostly in the Royal Library at Windsor Castle) give an accurate description of the Great Park as it was in the late eighteenth century. The two brothers were both founder members of the Royal Academy and made extensive changes to the Great Park. One of their masterpieces was the creation of Virginia Water Lake. By damming some of the nearby streams, they were able to construct a pondhead. The original pondhead was close to where the Leptis Magna ruins now stand, and extended to the headland on the opposite shore (now Botany Bay Point). Disaster overtook the Sandbys' creation in 1768, when torrential rain burst the damn and the whole lake was emptied, fish and all, and a nearby house swept away in the deluge. The brothers were undaunted and rebuilt the damn as it stands today with enormously solid and ruggedly romantic rocks from Bagshot Heath. By judicious flooding of additional land, the lake was extended to the dimensions we see today.

Drone photograph of the Leptis Magna ruins brought from the Libyan desert and reconstructed in the early nineteenth century at Virginia Water under the directorship of Wyatville. Corinthian columns support pedestals of stone — with half-broken columns, standing or lying on the ground. © Doug Harding.

Drone photograph taken from above the Lepta Magna ruins looking towards the Virginia Water Visitor Centre. © *Doug Harding.*

The Cascade at Virginia Water Lake — built by George III in the 1750s.

A view north from the most southerly tip of Virginia Water Lake towards Botany Bay Point. © *Doug Harding*.

One of the lake's most popular features, the waterfall (or Cascade), was built in 1790 using sarsen stones from the nearby Bagshot Heath. A grotto (cave) was also constructed, but the entrance has now been sealed off. Water exiting the lake forms the source of the River Bourne, which flows north east towards its confluence with the River Thames at Chertsey.[30]

Just south of Virginia Water, and outside the boundary of the Great Park, is Fort Belvedere – the little rococo castle on Shrub Hill, built by Wyatville in the Gothic Revival style. It became the home of King Edward VIII, who could sometimes be seen on the lake in his speedboat during the 1930s.[31] The relationship between Edward and Wallis Simpson blossomed here and the couple spent their first weekend at the fort at the end of January 1932. Edward signed his written abdication notices at Fort Belvedere on 10 December 1936 (witnessed by his three younger brothers)[32] and the following day he broadcast his message of abdication to the nation from Windsor Castle.

Looking west at a fiery orange sunset above the reed beds of Virginia Water Lake. © *Doug Harding*.

The Valley Gardens

The geology of the south-eastern part of the Great Park falls within the Bagshot Formation (formerly known as Bagshot Sands) – a classification which is derived from the nearby Bagshot Heath in Surrey. The ground underfoot consists of sandy, nutrient-poor, acid soil, which is virtually lime free. The types of plants that can be grown on such poor soil are limited, but the ground is suitable for rhododendrons, camellias, heathers and conifers.[33] In the late 1940s, Eric Savill, who was responsible for the management of the parkland, set about redeveloping the numerous sandy gullies that descend from Smith's Lawn to Virginia Water. The site was overgrown with trees and plants that quickly colonise acidic soil, such as birch and bracken. The clearance operation commenced with workers, recently demobbed from service against the Japanese, who dubbed the area 'Upper Burma'.[34]

One of the most spectacular parts of the Valley Gardens is The Punch Bowl, which is ablaze with colour in early May. Most of the 'Wilson Fifty' Kurume azaleas[35] can be found here. If you examine the Latin name of the 'azalea' plants that grace the woodland paths around The Punch Bowl, you will find that most are, in fact, a type of rhododendron.

Stunning display of spring azaleas in the Valley Gardens, Windsor Great Park.

The Punchbowl in full bloom, with its magnificent collection of rhododendrons and azaleas — best seen in May.

Bonfire shades of Acer Palmatum (Japanese maple) near the Valley Gardens.

The Totem Pole near Virginia Water Lake — a gift from the people of Canada to HM Queen Elizabeth II.

The Totem Pole

One of the most extraordinary sights in this section of the Great Park is the presence of a giant Totem Pole, which was a gift from the people of Canada to HM Queen Elizabeth II in June 1958.[36] Standing 100 feet high – one foot for every year – it marks the centenary of British Columbia, which was proclaimed a Crown Colony by Queen Victoria in November 1858. The pole was made from a 600 year-old Western Red Cedar and carved by Chief Mungo Martin, the most famous craftsman of this ancient art. There are ten figures on the totem pole, each creature representing the mythical ancestor of a clan[37]. Starting from the top these include: a Chief wearing his hat and robes, a Beaver, an Old Man, a Thunderbird, a Sea Otter holding a seal, a Raven, a Whale, A Woman surrounded by Sisiutl, a Halibut Man and a Cedar Man.[38]

The Savill Garden

The Savill Garden owes its name to its designer, Sir Eric Savill, who masterminded a series of interlinked gardens in the 1930s, with the support of King George V and Queen Mary. The gardens have always enjoyed royal patronage ever since, and many members of the Royal Family have planted trees here. The Rose Garden, which takes a fresh and contemporary approach to displaying roses, was opened by HM The Queen in 2010.

The visitor entrance to The Savill Building, Windsor Great Park, in late autumn twilight.

The Savill Garden is a place of constant discovery, and the interlocking gardens contain distinctive areas such as Spring Wood, The Summer Wood, The Hidden Gardens, The Summer Gardens, The Glades, Autumn Wood, The Azalea Walks and The New Zealand Garden.[39] The Garden mixes native and exotic species and has bred many important garden hybrids. Consciously emulating the great plant-hunters of a bygone age, the garden

Aerial view of the Golden Jubilee Garden with the Rose Garden behind it. © *Doug Harding*.

management search the globe for rare and unusual plant varieties. Each section of The Savill Garden has its own attractions, which are ever-changing, as each season brings new colour and interest to delight the visitor.

The Savill Building Visitor Centre was opened in the summer of 2006, and the wood used for the floor and roof was all harvested from the Windsor Crown Estate woodlands. The underside of the roof contains 400 larch trees from the estate and oak from sustainable woodlands of Cranbourne form the upper side.[40] The roof is a gridshell construction, supported by its own double curvature.

Drone photograph of The Savill Building with its gridshell construction and undulating roof, shaped like a leaf. © *Doug Harding*.

CHAPTER 4

WINDSOR EVENTS

A selection of some of the key Windsor events throughout the year are described below. A more comprehensive list of events and visitor attractions can be obtained from the Tourist Information Centre in the Windsor Royal Shopping Centre or by visiting the Royal Borough of Windsor & Maidenhead website.[1]

The Royal Windsor Horse Show

The Royal Windsor Horse Show began in 1943 to help raise funds for the war effort and the event has been staged every year since then.[2] It is the only horse show in the UK to host international competitions in show jumping, dressage, driving and endurance. The inaugural event – called the Windsor Horse and Dog Show – took place on Wednesday

Limbering up in the warm up arena for the Land Rover (grades A and B) Jumping competition during the 2018 Royal Windsor Horse Show.

26 May 1943 and was attended by all the key members of the Royal Family including King George VI, Queen Elizabeth (the Queen Mother) and the two young princesses, Elizabeth and Margaret. It helped the Royal Borough raise over £391,000 – enough money to buy 78 Typhoon fighter aircraft.

HM Queen Elizabeth II has always been a keen horsewoman and at the first show won the Pony and Dogcart class. In subsequent years Her Majesty has entered many homebred horses and ponies in various classes at the show. HRH Prince Philip, The Duke of Edinburgh, was a regular competitor in the International Driving Grand Prix, until his retirement from competition in 2003.

The Royal Windsor Horse Show takes place over five days in May in the grounds of the Home Park, Windsor Castle. Events are staged in five arenas (Castle, Copper Horse, Frogmore, Adelaide and Windsor Great Park/Home Park), and an extensive shopping village is provided for retail therapy. The show has grown in size and international importance and now encompasses a huge variety of equestrian sport - from carriage driving and show jumping competitions to extensive showing classes and equestrian displays. The competition programme is supplemented by a number of displays and evening performances such as the 'Musical Ride of the Household Cavalry Mounted Regiment', 'The Musical Drive of The King's Troop Royal Horse Artillery', 'The DAKS Pony Club Mounted Games' and 'The Shetland Pony Grand National'. The Royal Windsor Horse Show celebrated its 75th anniversary in May 2018.

Below left: A competitor clears a fence in the Castle Arena during The Walwyn Novice Jumping Championship (2018). Below right: Horse and rider in perfect harmony during a dressage event in 2015.

The Coaching Marathon (Class 72) in the Castle Arena during the 2011 Royal Windsor Horse Show.

One of the competitors warming up for a showing event in the Castle Arena during the 2011 Royal Windsor Horse Show.

The Windsor Festival

The roots of the festival date back to 1952, when the Dean of St George's Chapel, Windsor, and President of the Windsor and Eton Society, began staging the Windsor and Eton celebratory concerts.[3] Fifteen years later, the Dean met Yehudi Menuhin at a Royal Academy dinner, and the acclaimed violinist offered to put on concerts in St George's Chapel, Windsor Castle. Though their collaboration, an impressive evening of music took place in this esteemed venue.

The Dean began to realise the further potential of the castle as a place to stage an annual music or artistic festival – being inspired by similar festivals established in other cities. He imagined events extending from Windsor Castle to Eton, the Town Hall to the Theatre Royal and beyond.

Buskers on the Eton side of Windsor Bridge playing folk, roots and acoustic music.

Meanwhile, the former Director of the Edinburgh Festival and Menuhin's agent, was beginning to realise the potential of the area as a location to celebrate the arts. In 1968 he wrote to the Dean setting out his ideas and within a few months, a new charity – the Windsor Festival Society – was born.

In 2018, the autumn festival marked two significant centenaries: the end of the First World War and Women's Suffrage. These significant moments in the life of the nation were reflected through the festival's programme, with the literary series providing a platform to discuss the role of women. To mark the centenary of the Armistice of World War I, the Choir of St George's Chapel performed 'For the Fallen' which included works by composers associated with the Chapel. The sublime singing of the boy Choristers and Lay Clerks was a fitting memorial to the fallen of the Great War. Eton College's Great War Remembrance trail provided an opportunity to see art, memorials and treasured objects commemorating World War I. In addition to these two themes, the festival also featured classical and contemporary music concerts, talks, local art exhibitions and heritage walking tours of the Thames and Windsor Great Park.

Accordion player on Windsor Bridge entertaining the tourists with continental tunes.

The leading group of runners reach the end of the
Long Walk during the 2010 Windsor Half Marathon.

The Windsor Half Marathon

This event takes place in September each year, close to Windsor Castle and within the confines of Windsor Great Park.[4] It attracts competitors of all ages and abilities, from joggers to elite runners. The course begins and ends on the Long Walk and is comprised of two laps, one of approximately 4 miles, the other of around 7.5 miles with the remainder made up of a 1.5 mile section of the Long Walk at the start and end of the race. The total running distance adds up to 13.1 miles.

The ideal place for spectators to watch the race is at the end of the Long Walk near the Copper Horse. From here you can hear the muffled echos of the race commentary interspersed with rousing music, as the runners make their way to the start line. Groups of red deer trotting across the race route, against the stunning backdrop of Windsor Castle, add to the spectacle. When the race gets underway spectators clap and cheer as runners pass the end of the Long Walk. Away from the crowds, the scuffing of shoes on tarmac and the sound of heavy breathing reveal the challenge the competitors face. By the time the elite runners have completed the first lap of the Park, some joggers have only reached the end of the Long Walk. The winning time is usually under 1 hour 10 mins.

View from Snow Hill at the start of the 2010 Windsor Half Marathon with the double avenues of trees flanking the Long Walk draped in autumn livery.

It is worth noting that the 1908 Olympic Games established what is now the official distance for the Marathon. The race started near the East Terrace of Windsor Castle, and ended at the Olympic Stadium in Shepherd's Bush, London – thus creating the marathon distance of 26 miles and 385 yards. The Princess of Wales (later Queen Mary) started the race and Lord Desborough fired the starting pistol.[5] The route to the stadium took runners over Windsor Bridge, along Eton High Street and then into London via Slough.

The main field of runners reach the end of the Long Walk during the 2010 Windsor Half Marathon.

The Royal Windsor Triathlon

This event is the longest running triathlon in the UK, with a course that takes in the history and heritage of Windsor, and a field that has featured some of the biggest names in the sport. It begins early – around 6am on a June morning – with around 3000 competitors standing on the banks of the River Thames, wearing wet suits and swimming caps, poised to jump into the dark murky waters beneath. At this point in the race some of the swimmers may doubt their sanity. After the 1.5 km swim to Windsor Bridge and back to the event village, the competitors transition to the bike stage of the race and cycle 40 km

Competitors medal for the 2018 Royal Windsor Triathlon.

through the surrounding Berkshire countryside. The final transition involves a 10 km run (comprising 3 laps of the Long Walk up to the Albert Road), before heading for Windsor Castle and the finish line in Alexandra Gardens. There is also an option to do a Sprint version of the race, which is half the Olympic distance. Hundreds of spectators line the streets of Windsor to cheer on participants as they complete the challenge. The event includes electronic chip timing and a finisher's medal.[6]

Swimmers emerge exhausted and dripping from the Thames, near Deadwater Ait/Baths Island, ready for transition to the bike stage of the race in Alexandra Gardens.

Just over half way through the swim section of the Windsor Triathlon at 7am on a Sunday morning in June 2018.

Competitors in the final run stage of the 2018 Windsor Triathlon tackle the Long Walk, against the stunning backdrop of Windsor Castle.

CHAPTER 5
LITERARY WINDSOR

Many writers have been inspired by Windsor and the Great Park or have had associations with the town. This brief chapter includes a selection of writers, who either used Windsor as a setting for their work, or had associations with the Castle, the town, or the Court. For those seeking a more comprehensive analysis of Windsor's literary heritage, please refer to the Notes section.[1]

William Shakespeare

Shakespeare's Windsor-based comedy *'The Merry Wives of Windsor'* is the only play he set in England, and many locations mentioned can still be found around Windsor. The fourteenth century Garter Inn (now amalgamated with 'The White Hart' and re-named 'The Harte and Garter') was one of the settings for the opening scenes. The play may have been performed before Queen Elizabeth 1 and her Knights on St George's Day 1597, during the celebration of the Order of the Garter, although the evidence is not that compelling.

The fourteenth-century Garter Inn, used for the setting of '*The Merry Wives of Windsor*', was amalgamated with 'The White Hart' and re-named 'The Harte and Garter'.

Act 1, Scene III, takes place in a room in the Garter Inn, where Sir John Falstaff tells Pistol and Nym of his objective to 'cony-catch'[2] and falsely woo the wives of two leading Windsor merchants, Mistress Ford and Mistress Page, and extort money from them.[3] On hearing of his intentions, the wives devise plans to humiliate Falstaff. On reading his letter, Mistress Page exclaims: *'For revenged I will be, as sure as his guts are made of puddings'* and Mistress Ford remarks: *'What tempest I trow, threw this whale, with so many tuns of oil in his belly, ashore at Windsor?'*. Firstly, Falstaff is hidden in a large laundry basket and dumped into a ditch at Datchet Mead. Secondly, disguised as an elderly aunt, he is beaten out of the house. Finally, dressed as Herne the Hunter, he is invited

A portrait of Anne Page, in stained glass, on the staircase of 'The Harte and Garter' Hotel.

to meet Mistress Page at night in Windsor Forest, where he is pinched and taunted by children dressed as fairies. According to folklore, Herne was a keeper who went mad after being gored by a stag. He is said to have run naked through the Forest with a pair of antlers tied to his head, before hanging himself on a tree in the Home Park.[4]

The following phrases from the play have now passed into common usage: 'the world's my oyster', 'as (good) luck would have it' and 'laughing stock'.

A portrait of Sir John Falstaff, in stained glass, quaffing a tankard of ale.

John Evelyn

John Evelyn was a writer, gardener and diarist, whose personal motto was *'Omnia explorate; meliora retinete'* ('Explore everything; keep the better'; based on 1 Thessalonians 5:21).[5] He was born in Wotton (near Dorking, Surrey) into a family whose wealth was largely founded on gunpowder production. As a prolific author, he wrote books on subjects as diverse as theology, politics, horticulture, architecture and vegetarianism. He was known for his knowledge of trees, and his treatise, *'Sylva, or A Discourse of Forest-Trees'*, was written as an encouragement to landowners to plant trees to provide timber for England's burgeoning navy[6]. Evelyn was a wealthy Royalist and in favour with King Charles II, and witnessed the transformation of Windsor Castle after the ravages of the Civil War. On a visit to Windsor in June 1654, he saw *'the Castle and Chapel of St. George, where they have laid our blessed Martyr, King Charles, in the vault just before the altar'[7]*, and walking on the terrace he thought that *'Eton, with the park, meandering Thames, and sweet meadows, yield one of the most delightful prospects'*.

The church of St John the Evangelist, Wotton, where John Evelyn is buried in the Evelyn Chapel.

The grand demesne of Eton College, the meandering Thames and the Buckinghamshire countryside, as viewed from the Round Tower of Windsor Castle.

He was also responsible for discovering, Grinling Gibbons, the master wood carver, *'by mere accident'*, and introduced him to King Charles II. Whilst walking near a solitary thatched house in his parish (near Sayes Court), Evelyn looked in through a window, and saw a young man carving an elaborate copy of a Tintoretto Crucifixion.[8] He went in, enquired the cost and made his acquaintance. As he explains in his diary entry of 18 January 1671: *'Of this young artist, together with my manner of finding him out, I acquainted the King, and begged that he would give me leave to bring him and his work to Whitehall. This was the first notice his Majesty ever had of Mr. Gibbon'*[9] .Wren and Evelyn subsequently introduced Gibbons to King Charles II, who gave the wood carver his first commission, which is still residing in the dining room of Windsor Castle. Some years later, when Evelyn saw the incomparable carvings that Gibbons had produced in Windsor Castle, he was justifiably proud of his 'discovery'.

Many would point to Evelyn's diary as his greatest gift to posterity. It was discovered by chance, a hundred years after his death, by a librarian visiting Wotton House[10]. Evelyn was also a contemporary of Samuel Pepys and the two men knew each other well, but were never aware they were both diarists.

Jonathan Swift

Jonathan Swift is best known for his novel *Gulliver's Travels*, a book that satirized eighteenth century politicians and their ideologies. He came to Windsor Castle in 1711 to make himself known to court circles, in the hope of winning the favour of Queen Anne, and being rewarded with an English Deanery.[11] During his three years there, he either stayed in lodgings at the Castle or travelled down for the day. He also wrote a series of letters to 'Stella' – a girl he had tutored and mentored, when working at Moor

The double avenue of plane and chestnut trees than line the Long Walk.

Park, and with whom he maintained a close (but ambiguous) relationship for the rest of his life. Regarding Queen Anne's passion for hunting and riding, he wrote in July 1711: *'She hunts in a chaise with one horse … and drives furiously, like Jehu, and is a mighty hunter, like Nimrod'.*[12] Writing to Stella again in September 1711, he remarked[13]: *'I take all opportunities of walking; and we have a delicious park here just joining to the Castle, and an avenue in the great park very wide and two miles long, set with a double row of elms on either side. Were you ever at Windsor?'* In the end Swift never acquired his English Deanery, but in 1713 he became Dean of St Patrick's Cathedral in Dublin, where he raised his literary voice in protest at English injustice and neglect.

Looking towards 'The Copper Horse' from the 'Double Gates', along a snow-covered Long Walk.

Alexander Pope

Pope's literary association with Windsor is the eighteenth century topographical poem *Windsor Forest*, which incorporates panegyric, pastoral, historical and political elements into its 422 lines.[14] Pope's family were Catholic and they moved to Binfield, on the fringes of Windsor Forest, to escape the prejudice they had encountered in London. The poet regarded his childhood in Windsor Forest as the happiest time of his life, and it is thought that he composed the majority of the poem when he was only fifteen.[15] The poem opens with the following lines: *'Thy forest, Windsor! and thy green retreats / At once the monarch's and the muse's seats.'*[16]

Pope uses the Garden of Eden as a metaphor for Windsor Forest because he sees it as a perfect creation. He declares that Queen Anne is like the goddess Diana because of her strength and hunting skills and calls the River Thames *'great father of the British floods!'* Some other memorable lines include: *'Thy trees, fair Windsor! now shall leave their woods / And half thy forests rush into thy floods'* and *'The time shall come, when, free as seas or wind / Unbounded Thames shall flow for all mankind.'* The above lines refer to Britain's wealth of timber (used for ship construction), which helped establish its trade links around the world.[17]

A tiled replica of Hollar's seventeenth century engraving of Windsor Castle, in the covered walkway alongside 'The King and Castle' pub.

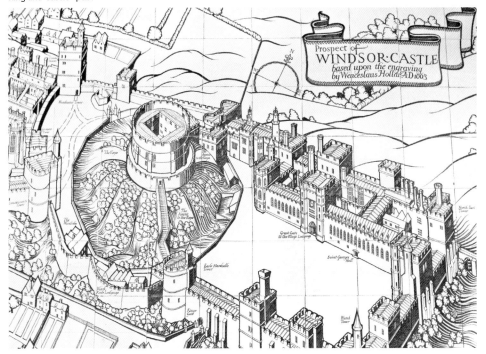

A group of red deer, near The Long Walk, keep a wary eye out for photographers. The deer are descendants of a small number of stags and hinds re-introduced from Balmoral into the Great Park in 1979, which have successfully multiplied over the last forty years.

H.G.Wells

H.G.Wells was a prolific writer in many genres, but is best known for his scientific romances, *The War of the Worlds*, *The Time Machine* and *The Invisible Man*. He has often been referred to as 'the father of science fiction'. His connection with Windsor began as a boy. His mother's cousin (Uncle Tom) ran The Royal Oak public house, opposite Windsor and Eton Riverside station, and later, Surly Hall – an inn with lawns running down to the river.[18] As a boy, young Bertie (H.G. Wells), stayed there during the summer holidays, and leant to punt and row on the river. When he was thirteen, it was decided that he should follow his brothers into the drapery business. Uncle Tom found him a trial placement at Rodgers and Denyer in Windsor High Street.[19] As an apprentice Bertie worked a 72 hour week and earned sixpence, plus his keep. His job was at the cash desk keeping the books, but the poor food and the long and dreary hours were not appealing to his creative nature. Bertie escaped to Surly Hall as often as he could and eventually left the drapery business to become a pupil-teacher. Two of his later novels of social satire, *The History of Mr Polly* and *Kipps,* are inspired by his experiences in the drapery business. Windsor Castle also makes a startling appearance (or rather a disappearance) in his 1923 Utopian fantasy *Men like Gods.*

The Royal Oak pub, opposite Windsor and Eton Riverside Station, now re-named 'The Royal Windsor'.

A plaque marks the spot where H.G.Wells worked as a drapers' apprentice.

The 'Glorious Britain' shop now occupies the premises where Rodgers and Denyer once stood.

Edward Thomas

Edward Thomas was a poet, novelist, essayist and literary critic. He was already a seasoned writer by the outbreak of World War I, having published widely as a literary critic and biographer, as well as a topographical writer about the countryside (*The South Country*, *In Pursuit of Spring*).[20] Encouraged by the American poet, Robert Frost, he began writing poetry in December 1914.[21] In the next 30 months – as if writing against a deadline – he produced a constant stream of poetry, sometimes writing more than a poem a day. In 1910 he was commissioned to write a short guide to Windsor Castle for Blackie's Beautiful England Series.[22] He took on the job in January 1910, for completion the following month. It involved rapid research in the British Library Reading Room and a brief visit to Windsor. Although the outcome – *Windsor Castle*[23] – is considered to be a minor work, Thomas's poetic imagination shines forth from its 56 pages. The scene is set in the opening paragraph, where: *'Seen from the flat meadows of Clewer on a moist morning, when thrushes are singing in the elms, Windsor Castle rises up like a cloud in the east.'* The view shifts to the near neighbourhood, where: *'Nowhere are elmy meadows, mistletoed poplars, willowy serpentining brooks, sweeter than at Datchet'.* Next, the castle's position gets his attention: *'It stands upon a single blunt cone of chalk projecting through the clay of the surrounding low lands'*, and then the view from the Clewer footpath to Eton Chapel: *'with its high dark windows among poplars and serrated roofs in a sky of grey satin, and to the right the closely gathered huge bulk of the Castle above the small town'.* The splendour of St George's Chapel is extolled: *'It is exquisite and elaborate. It holds and embalms the sunlight'.* There are touches of dry, sardonic humour, throughout: *'Doubtless the jackdaws, gliding straight out into the clear air from the Round Tower, have been there since Crécy, but the stonework is new.'* Since his death, at the Battle of Arras, in April 1917, Edward Thomas's reputation as a poet has grown steadily, and his work is now regarded as one of the foundation stones of modern British poetry.

Photograph of Edward Thomas at Steep (circa 1914), taken by Maitland Radford.

CHAPTER 6

THE RIVER THAMES

'Once upon a time a Queen of England was rowed down the silver Thames to the sweet low sound of the flute'.

Richard Jefferies[1]

The nineteenth century politician John Burns once described the River Thames as 'liquid history',[2] a phrase that acknowledges the central role the river has played in the life of the capital city – both economic, social, political and cultural. It has been an important artery between London and the Heart of England since earliest times, and vital to the transportation of goods and personnel. The Romans gave the river its name[3], Tamesis – a combination of Isis, the old name for the river from its source to Dorchester, and Thame, the tributary it meets near Dorchester. The Saxons invaded

Windsor Castle rises like a cloud above the silvery Thames – once described by Winston Churchill as 'the silver artery of the Empire'.

Cruise passengers board the *Windsor Monarch* — one of the French Brothers' fleet, with a very large upper deck, making it ideal for parties with a disco. The cruise boat is capable of accommodating up to 100 people on the wooden-decked dance floor! On the opposite bank, canoeists glide past Eton Rowing Club.

England along the Thames and the Normans built major fortresses along its banks. It is likely that Windsor grew from a Saxon settlement into a town due to the proximity of the river. Before the Norman Conquest, the right of regulating the river fell to the Crown, and in 1065, Edward the Confessor decreed that 'if mills, fisheries or other works were constructed which hindered navigation, they should be destroyed'.[4] But as Hilaire Belloc pointed out, a river has a second topographical and historic function (in addition to navigation): as an obstacle, a defence and a boundary[5]. In so far as it is an obstacle, it is also a means of defence and the point at which the river is crossed is certain to become a point of strategic and often commercial significance. Windsor certainly offered that opportunity, and the steep platform of chalk, rising out of the damp clay, on the south bank of the Thames, was the place the Conqueror chose to build his castle.

The Thames has been described as 'The King of Island Rivers'[6]. Although the Severn is the longest river in the United Kingdom, the Thames is the longest river (entirely) in England: the distance from source to sea being 215 miles. The tidal reaches of the Thames stretch from Teddington Lock to the Estuary, with the tide rising and falling twice a day, by up to 7 metres.

River Craft and Cruises

The non-tidal Thames around Windsor, with its great sweeping bends and sinuous curves, attracts a variety of pleasure craft, including motor cruisers, narrowboats, rowing boats, canoes and house boats. French Brothers run regular short cruises along the River Thames from Windsor. The 40 minute round trip[7] to Boveney Lock, passes Firework Eyot, the Brocas Meadows, Jacob's Island, Deadwater Eyot/Baths Island, Windsor Railway Bridge (designed by Brunel), Queen Elizabeth Bridge and the Royal Windsor Racecourse.

Cruise passengers disembark from the *Windsor Sceptre*, as swans gather around the landing stage waiting to be fed.

The two hour round trip[8] takes visitors further upstream to Dorney Lake,[9] a world-class, flat-water rowing lake selected to host the kayak and rowing events at the 2012 Olympic and Paralympic Games. The 2.2 km, eight-lane course, was constructed to International Standards by Eton College Boat Club, who use it as a training venue all year round. The cruise continues to Bray via Windsor Marina, Queen's Eyot, Bray Marina and Monkey Island. Here the crew wind ship and return to Windsor, aided by the current, which makes journey times slightly shorter.

Rowing boats for hire on the Thames promenade.

Rowers on Dorney Lake (owned and managed by Eton College) — used to host the kayak and rowing events at the 2012 Olympic and Paralympic Games.

Weirs, Locks and Flood Relief Schemes

In the Middle Ages, the fall on the Thames in its middle and upper sections was used to drive watermills for the production of flour, paper and other industrial products. This involved the construction of weirs to divert water into the mills. The weirs, however, presented an obstacle to navigation, and in the seventeenth century, locks were built alongside the weirs to enable river traffic to move from one level of river reach to another.[10]

Yellow motor boats for hire on the Thames promenade.

Narrowboat moored up on the Thames, near Jacobs Island, with colourful potted plants on the roof.

Romney Lock dates from the 1790s and is around 800 metres downstream of Windsor Bridge on the stretch of river that loops north, skirting The Home Park. The eponymous weir is some distance upstream at the end of Romney Island and runs across the river to Cutlers Ait. The Castle's electricity supply is now powered by two giant hydro-electric turbines (Archimedes' screws) at Romney Weir, which generate 200 to 300 kWh when the river is in good flow; this is one of a number of renewable energy initiatives that have been introduced by the Royal Household.[11] The next lock upstream of Windsor Bridge is Boveney Lock, first built in 1838 by the Thames Navigation Commission. It is situated on the 'Buckinghamshire' bank, opposite Windsor Racecourse and close to Eton Wick.

The towns of Maidenhead, Windsor and Eton, and nearby villages on the banks of the River Thames, have a long history of flooding. Weirs are used to maintain river levels regardless of how much water is in the river system[12] and provide a constant river level for navigation under flood or drought conditions. At times of flood and heavy rain extra sluices can be opened to pass more water downstream, and prevent the river from bursting its banks. In times of drought, the weir slows down the amount of water flowing to the next reach, ensuring levels are sufficiently deep for navigation above the tideway.

Rivercraft on the Thames near Romney Island.

Large river craft (*Magna Carta*) moored up along the south bank of the Thames.

In times of prolonged torrential rain or during a sudden spring thaw, the weirs and locks may be unable to cope with the volume of water in the river system and then flooding will occur. The worst flooding Windsor has experienced occurred in March 1947 and a detailed account of the disaster has been written.[13] Although there was considerable public pressure on the relevant authorities to stop a similar flood happening again, it took years for a suitable solution to be found and financed. All methods of flood relief were considered (by the Environmental Agency) including storage, dredging and embankments (dams), before it was decided that the best solution was to construct a Flood Relief Channel, known as the Jubilee River, from upstream of Maidenhead to downstream of Windsor. The 7 mile channel runs along the east side of the River Thames, leaving the river at Boulter's Weir and re-joining it at Black Potts Viaduct just downstream of Windsor.[14] It has a trapezoidal cross-section with a bottom width of around 30 metres, and was designed to look and function as a natural living river, containing water all year round. The Jubilee River was opened in July 2002 by HRH The Duke of York. However, in the early months of 2014, some Ham Island and Wraysbury residents, claimed that the Jubilee River had increased the height of the flooded Thames in their neighbourhoods,[15] with water levels unprecedented since 1947. Since the channel affords no protection to communities downstream of the scheme, there are plans to extend the Jubilee River to Wraysbury and Old Windsor in future.

Wooden footbridge over the Jubilee River.

A bevy of swans (and other water fowl) on the Thames promenade at Windsor.

Thames Bridges (from Datchet to Clewer)

Just upstream of Ham Island, where the river performs one of its spectacular horseshoe bends,[16] is Albert Bridge. The cast-iron structure carries the B3021 across the Thames between Old Windsor and Datchet, and was completed in 1850-51. Prince Albert is said to have had a hand in its design. In 1914, the bridge was damaged and a hole appeared in the middle of the carriageway. The rebuilding plans ran into difficulties, which accounted for a delay of around ten years before the bridge could be rebuilt in 1927. The new design had two reinforced concrete river arches and three flood arches on the Berkshire bank (retained from the original structure). Three half turrets were also added, adjacent to the main arches, to provide pedestrian refuges.[17] By 2003, several accidents had taken their toll on the bridge balustrades and complete renewal of the structure was required.[18] Pink balustrading was used to replace the original design and high kerbs added to prevent vehicles mounting the pavement.

Its companion bridge (Victoria Bridge) – around 2 km upstream – was built at the same time and paid for, in part, by the Windsor, Staines and Richmond Railway Company. Since the new line from Staines to Windsor would need to be built across The Home Park (in the grounds of Windsor Castle) the railway company was required to seek the permission of Parliament and Queen Victoria in 1847.[19] This was granted in 1848 in return for a substantial contribution towards the costs of a new road and a river bridge. Due to problems arising from the Second World War, when a string of tanks crossed the bridge, overloading and seriously damaging it, the bridge was closed for repairs in the 1960s. The main arch was replaced by two high-tensile steel ribs carrying vertical pillars which support a reinforced concrete deck. The bridge was re-opened in 1967, and under the terms of the original contract, British Rail was required to pay a substantial contribution to the costs of repair.

The *Lady Margaret Anne* returning from the upper Thames near Windsor Race Course.

The *Queen of the Thames* glides past Romney Island on its return journey to Windsor.

Black Potts Railway Bridge carries the line from Staines to Windsor across the Thames, on the reach between Old Windsor Lock and Romney Lock, before terminating at Windsor and Eton Riverside Station. The bridge's name was taken from a fishing house used by Sir Isaac Walton and his friend Sir Henry Wotton, the Provost of Eton. The London and South Western Railway line was expected to be the first railway service into Windsor, but when the track was laid two of the piers subsided (one of the columns resting on the river bed moved, and a supporting girder cracked).[20] So that instead of reaching Windsor on 9 August 1849, the first train did not leave

Black Potts Railway Viaduct (and weir), which carries the South Western line over the Jubilee River to Windsor and Eton Riverside Station.

Waterloo until 1 December 1849 – two months after the Great Western Railway had reached Windsor and Eton Central Station on 8 October 1849.[21] The original bridge had four spans with vertically ribbed spandrels and decorative cast iron parapets. Both these features were removed in 1954, vastly altering the appearance of the structure. Immediately to the east of the bridge is the Black Potts Railway Viaduct. This was added to provide substantial protection when the Jubilee River was constructed, as the outfall of this channel passes through the brick arches of the existing Victorian viaduct, just downstream of the bridge.

View of the Côte Brasserie restaurant (formerly the 'House on the Bridge') taken from Windsor Bridge.

Windsor Bridge is now a pedestrian crossing over the Thames which links Thames Street, Windsor to Eton High Street. The original wooden bridge on this site was built in the twelfth century and historical records indicate that in 1242, permission was granted for oak trees to be felled in Windsor Forest for the purpose of building a new bridge over the Thames. Construction of the bridge, as we know it today, began in 1822, with Charles Hollis as engineer.[22] It was designed as three cast iron arches, each of seven ribs, supported by two colossal granite pillars (and abutments), set deep into the river bed. Work was completed on 1st June 1824, at a cost of £15,000, and for many years afterwards a toll was charged for its use. Due to a series of public protests, the tolls were eventually scrapped in 1898. Although the bridge had a weight limit, it was never designed to take the weight and speed of modern traffic, and as the new century

View of Windsor Bridge and Castle taken from the Eton side of the river.

progressed it began to show signs of wear. The last motorised vehicle crossed the bridge on 10 April 1970, and from then on the bridge was restricted to pedestrian and cycle traffic. The bridge undertook a load assessment in 2000 when it was concluded that although the main arch ribs were generally sound, 40% of the spandrels were cracked or sheared. Restoration work began in February 2002, when new parapets and integral lighting were added. The project was completed in time for the Golden Jubilee celebrations in June 2002, when HM The Queen re-opened the bridge and unveiled a plaque commemorating the refurbishment.

The *Bray Royale* about to berth near Firework Ait, about 150 metres upstream of Windsor Bridge. The Ait is the smallest island on the Thames with an official map-published name. An account of Eton life from the 1840s postulates that Percy Bysshe Shelley, when at Eton (in 1805), would have taken his skiff across to the 'eyot which then served for fireworks'.

Windsor Railway Bridge is the world's oldest wrought-iron railway bridge still in regular use,[23] and carries the branch line over the River Thames on the reach between Romney Lock and Boveney Lock. It was designed by Isambard Kingdom Brunel in 1849, as a 'bow and string' style structure, which provided two bays for the original GWR tracks. The single-span design, is approached from the north on a brick viaduct more than 1 km long, and crosses the Thames at an angle of 60 degrees.[24] The track on the upstream side was removed in the 1960s, when the line was modernised.

The *Windsor Royal* passes under Brunel's 'bow and string' style railway bridge.

The Queen Elizabeth II Bridge, opened in July 1966, and carries the A332 (Windsor and Eton Bypass) over the Thames, upstream of Windsor. It is a cantilever bridge with three spans, made of reinforced concrete. The outer box sections rest on two piers and are anchored at the abutments to form cantilevers that extend towards each other across the river, providing two-thirds of the main span. The remaining third consists of a central span suspended between the free ends of the cantilevers.[25]

View of Windsor Castle from a snow-covered Brocas, set against a dramatic purple sky. © *Doug Harding*.

CHAPTER 7
WINDSOR AND ETON WALKS

The following four walks provide a taster of Windsor, Eton and the Great Park, both on and off the tourist trail. All routes are circular and range from 1 to 8 miles. Although a detailed description of each route is given and a sketch map provided, it is advisable to take with you a smartphone with Google maps and an OS map of the area (160 Explorer).

The band of the Household Calvary parade past Queen Victoria's Statue as they return to barracks after Guard Mount.

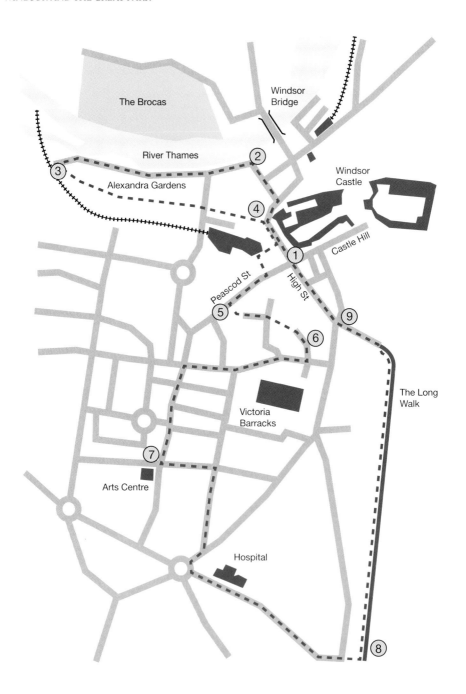

WALK 1: Windsor Town Trail

Start: Queen Victoria Statue, Castle Hill; Start reference: SU 968769;
length = 3 ¾ miles (5.9 km); this route follows part of 'The Queen's Walkway'
(an official guidebook is available from the Tourist Information Centre).

1. With your back to the Queen Victoria Statue at the foot of Castle Hill, bear right along Thames Street past the entrance to the Windsor Royal Shopping centre. Follow the road as it swings sharp right past the Curfew Tower. Pass the Theatre Royal and the newly erected security barriers and follow the road as it veers left past the bronze statue of Prince Christian Victor. Cross the Dachet Road via the Pelican pedestrian crossing and keep ahead along the cobbled street past the Sir Christopher Wren Hotel and Spa.

2. Just before Windsor Bridge, go left down a flight of steps and continue along the Thames promenade, with the river on your right. Pass the landing stage for the French Brothers Cruises, a small wooded island (Firework Ait) and a collection of self-drive motor boats for hire. Pass another larger wooded ait (Jacob's Island / Snap Ait) and Café Barry, which serves a good selection of refreshments. The promenade passes under some weeping willows where Brunel's 'Bow and String' railway bridge is visible in the distance.

The *Windsor Regent* cruise boat moored up on the Thames promenade.

3. Continue past another larger island (Deadwater Ait/ Baths Island) and when you see a full-sized replica of a Hawker Hurricane aircraft, go left across road and left again into the park (Alexandra Gardens). When the path splits, branch left along path parallel to road. Pass a large seating area around an oak tree and then cut across greensward to the right of the bandstand. Exit park and keep ahead across road into The Goswells. Continue along wooded avenue with a maze and tennis courts on the right and a fountain and bowling green on the left. Continue up flight of steps alongside the King and Castle (Wetherspoons pub) and past a large tiled replica of Hollar's seventeenth century etching 'Prospect of Windsor Castle'.

Full-size replica of the Hawker Hurricane fighter aircraft unveiled on the Thames promenade (near Alexandra Gardens) in July 2012.

This ornamental fountain, inspired by the crown jewels, was constructed in The Goswells to mark the Queen's Diamond Jubilee in 2012.

4. When you emerge from the covered walkway opposite Windsor Castle, go right along Thames Street, past McDonald's and The Duchess of Cambridge pub. Take the first right into the Windsor Royal Shopping Centre. After passing Café Rouge and the Tourist Information Centre, go immediately left (before the French Connection) down a flight of steps and along a narrow alleyway (Goswell Hill). At the next junction, go right along Peascod Street, past Marks and Spencer, Boots, Waterstones and the Daniel department store.

Part of the original GWR tower in Windsor and Eton Central Station. The original station was completed in 1897 in time for Queen Victoria's Diamond Jubilee celebrations.

5. When you see an information board and semi-circular seating area, go left (before Paperchase) down a narrow alley (Peascod Place). Bear left, before Windsor Library car park, along Mellor Walk and then keep ahead across road into Bachelor's Acre. Just after a children's play area, cut half right across greensward to view 'The Windsor Lady' – a sculpture which depicts The Queen and her Corgis.

The bronze sculpture 'The Windsor Lady' depicts HM The Queen in informal dress surrounded by six Corgis. This gift from a Maidenhead sculptor, Lydia Karpinska, was installed in Bachelor's Acre to mark the Queen's Diamond Jubilee in 2012.

6. Follow hedge line to exit park near the Jubilee Obelisk. Go right along Victoria Street, pas¤ the red brick perimeter wall of the Victoria Barracks and a grey Baptist Chapel, until you reach a set of traffic lights and The Queen Victoria pub. Go left here along St Leonards Road – a continuation of Peascod Street and similarly bedecked with red, white and blue Union Jack bunting. Pass Templars Hall and Holy Trinity Garrison Church on the right.

Windsor's Arts Centre in St Leonards Road, previously known as 'The Firestation', now re-opened as 'The Old Court' (the building's original name).

7. Just before you reach the Old Court Arts Centre (formerly called the Firestation), go left along Grove Road. Take the next right along Alexandra Road and continue to the end, passing All Saints Church (designed by Thomas Hardy, when an apprentice architect). Go right here and then left at roundabout along Osborne Road. Pass the Princess Margaret Hospital and when you draw level with the next large roundabout, note the sculpture of the Windsor Greys on the traffic island. Carefully cross Kings Road and maintain direction over greensward and under the double avenue of trees to reach The Long Walk.

A life-size bronze sculpture of a pair of Windsor Greys, Daniel and Storm (the horses who draw the royal carriages on state occasions) installed on a roundabout at the junction of Albert and King's Road

8. Go left here towards the South Front of Windsor Castle, and just before you reach it, follow driveway as it swings left, past The Two Brewers Pub, along Park Street.

9. When the road forks, bear half left past the Irish Guards statue and up the High Street. Continue past the Parish Church and The Guildhall to the Queen Victoria Statue, where the walk began.

The Queen's Walkway was established to mark the occasion of HM The Queen becoming Britain's longest reigning monarch. It was officially opened on The Queen's 90th Birthday (21 April 2016). This is one of the plaques that mark the 6.3 km self-guided trail, which link 63 of Windsor's best-loved attractions.

A group stroll down the Long Walk towards the South Front of Windsor Castle.

WALK 2: Windsor Great Park

Start: The Savill Garden car park; Grid reference: SU 977706; Postcode: TW20 0UJ;
Length = 8 miles (13 km)

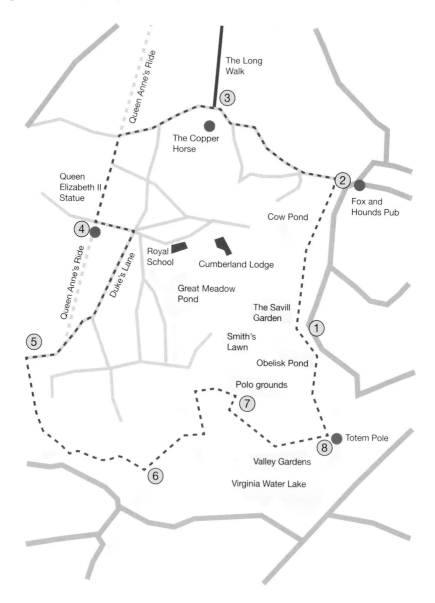

1. Proceed to main entrance of the Savill Building and then bear right along tarred drive, past the coach park and a line of garages. When the drive swings left, keep ahead along unmetalled track with rhododendron hedges on both sides. Pass Cow Pond on left (covered in water lilies) and continue to end of avenue.

2. When you reach the lodge at Bishopsgate, bear left along tarmac drive. Take next right at road junction near the Royal Lodge (pink building), and enter the Deer Park via the green metal gate. Proceed along wide tarred drive through a vaste and magnificent expanse of parkland. In due course, Windsor Castle may be glimpsed through the trees to your right. Cross bridge over dried-up stream and when you reach The Long Walk, savour the sensational views on offer towards Windsor Castle (2.5 miles away) along this iconic tree-lined route – a roofscape like no other in the world.

Family group near the Cumberland Obelisk — a few hundred metres away from the entrance to The Savill Building.

Group of walkers, from the WiSy Meetup Group, taking a breather near the Copper Horse statue.

Procession of carriages pass the end of the Long Walk near Snow Hill, en route for the change-over point in Duke's Lane.

3. To your left, an equestrian statue of King George III on a rocky plinth (The Copper Horse) crowns the summit of Snow Hill. Maintain direction along tarred drive which gradually swings left to follow an undulating course. Go through a green deer gate and then fork immediately right. As the road continues, the vista of Windsor Castle, appears and disappears behind pockets of woodland. Just before a house, bear left along a wide grassy walkway (Queen Anne's Ride). Pass a large millstone, set on its side, which was quarried in Derbyshire and brought here in 1992 to mark the re-planting of Queen Anne's Ride with 1000 oak trees. Cross another drive and proceed up the wide walkway, lined with oaks, towards an equestrian statue on the horizon.

Walkers with parasol stroll along Queen Anne's Ride, with equestrian statue in background.

4. This statue of Queen Elizabeth II was erected in 2002 to mark her Golden Jubilee and large clumps of mistletoe can be seen in the lime trees around it. Bear left here along drive and when you reach a major junction, go right along Duke's Lane. Most of the trees that line the lane are oaks, and some have circular grey signs signifying when the tree was planted. The grass on both sides is immaculately manicured, but for most of the year the lane is not widely used, compared to other areas of the Park. But for one week in June (Royal Ascot) crowds of people appear from all directions, all heading for the change-over point, where The Royal Family and their guests transfer from cars to horse-drawn carriages, as they make their way to Ascot racecourse. Ignore first turning on left (which is out of bounds to the public), and continue along lane, which dips downhill, then rises again.

HM The Queen and HRH The Duke of Edinburgh travel through Windsor Great Park on the final day of Royal Ascot 2010.

HM The Queen seated in an Ascot landau at the change-over point in Duke's Lane, on the second day of Royal Ascot 2015. She is wearing 'Prince Albert's Sapphire Brooch' — a large oblong sapphire brooch surrounded by twelve diamonds, which was given to Queen Victoria by Prince Albert on the day before their wedding.

5. Take the next left (before Prince Consort's Gate), along a sandy horse track (where cycling is not permitted). The track proceeds through mixed woodland and crosses over a number of dried up streams, before reaching a brick bridge over a stream. Leave the horse track here and bear left along a wide grassy ride. As you proceed, a large body of water (Virginia Water Lake) will appear on the right hand side.

6. When the grassy ride ends (near the Five Arch Bridge), go left along road (with a horse track alongside it). In due course, the road swings round to the right, and crosses two speed bumps, near Johnson's Pond. (Beyond the iron fence to your right the water cascades over a waterfall and into Virginia Water Lake.) Keep on the road, which climbs steeply up Breakheart Hill, with white stones lining the route. At the crest of the hill, go right past the polo grounds on Smith's Lawn and the Guards Polo Club. You may be fortunate enough to come when a polo match is in session, which the public are welcome to watch, free of charge.

This 100 foot Totem Pole was erected here in 1958 to mark the centenary of British Columbia as a Crown Colony.

7. After passing the Club store and the main entrance to the Club (which features a polo horse sculpture), bear sharp right across the greensward towards an information board for The Valley Gardens. When you reach it, keep ahead for 30 metres, then go left through a gate into the Heather Garden. Keep on sandy path that wends its way through heather beds of Erica Vagans 'Yellow John' and dwarf conifers (such as Thuja Orientalis). Every now and then there are benches provided to rest your weary limbs. Exit Heather Garden via gate and keep ahead through picnic area, following signs for the Totem Pole. If you wish to make a detour to The Punchbowl (with its spectacular display of azaleas and rhododendrons in Spring), follow signs off to the right (just after the mobile café). To continue walk, carry on along wide track, which gradually descends to the Totem Pole – an unmistakable 100 foot pole of red cedar, with highly ornamented carvings, which rises dramatically above the landscape.

8. Bear left here and follow tarmac road that climbs steeply, and then swings left and then right. At junction, keep ahead, in the direction of Savill Garden. If you come in the autumn, the trees here are a riot of colour. Continue downhill along the right hand edge of Obelisk Pond and follow the rising path that swings left, past the Cumberland Obelisk and leads back to the Savill Garden Building.

Spectacular autumn display of *Liriodendron Tulipifera* (American tulip tree) near Obelisk Pond.

Obelisk monument, built in the early 1750s by King George II, to honour the military successes of his son, William, Duke of Cumberland. As Ranger of Windsor Great Park, the Duke created Virginia Water Lake, commissioned many buildings and bridges, and planted substantial collections of native and exotic trees.

WALK 3: Windsor, Eton and the Thames Path

Start: Thames Street near Windsor Bridge; Start reference: SU 968772;
length = 5 ¼ miles (8.3 km)

1. Proceed across Windsor Bridge, pausing to take in the iconic views on offer. Glance down at the swirling Thames, noting the debris of twigs, leaves and blossom carried downstream by the flowing current. The bridge is the umbilical cord that connects Windsor to Eton. (Before 1974, the river divided the counties of Berkshire and Buckinghamshire, but now both sides of the river are in Berkshire.) When you reach the Eton bank, take the first left along Brocas Street, passing to the left of the Waterman's Arms and onto The Brocas. Keep following the obvious path across the greensward with the Thames on your left hand side. There is always a hive of activity on the water with regular river cruises along this stretch of the Thames. In the airspace above, jets bound for Heathrow fly over the castle in a never-ending line. (An American tourist was once overheard saying: 'Aww... the castle sure looks dandy, but why the heck did they build it so close to an airport!'). When the meadow ends, look left to catch a glimpse of a replica Hawker Hurricane, on the opposite river bank. Continue along the Thames Path passing under Brunel's 'bow and string' railway bridge which carries the line from Slough to Windsor over the river. When a large boat passes listen out for the loud lapping of water as the waves rebound off the riverbank. To your right is the 19th century railway viaduct that carries the line over the flood plains of Eton. Cross two footbridges then pass under a concrete cantilever bridge that carries the A332 dual carriageway over the river.

The towns of Windsor and Eton are essentially contiguous — joined together by the umbilical cord of the bridge.

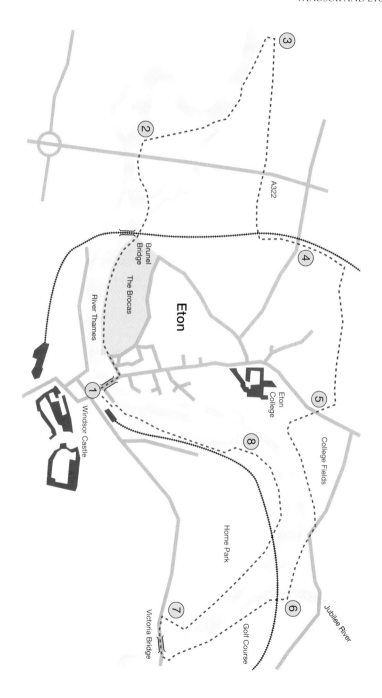

The Brocas, Eton – a magnificent riverside meadow bedecked in autumn livery.

A cruise boat passes under Brunel's 'bow and string' wrought iron railway bridge en route for the Upper Thames.

2. Soon afterwards take the white gravel path that deviates away from the river and joins it further upstream (effectively cutting the corner). Joggers, walkers and cyclists all use this path. After crossing a footbridge, open fields appear on the right (and beyond them the Eton Wick Road). Keep going until you pass a wooden bench on a concrete plinth, with a memorial stone beside it. This is the bathing place called 'Athens' once used by Eton College boys. The white railings on the opposite bank are part of Windsor Racecourse.

The Round Tower soars majestically above the Thames.

3. Look out for an inverted green triangle on a pole, then bear right, away from the river, along a narrow field path. At next fingerpost, go right again along a broad field path, heading back on yourself, towards the Castle. Follow field path as it tunnels under the busy A332 dual carriageway, through one of the graffiti-covered white arches. Cross meadow, then pass under arch of railway viaduct. Go left and follow tarred path to a road, with allotments on left.

The bathing place called 'Athens' (opposite Windsor Race Course) — once used by Eton school boys for swimming. George Orwell (aka Eric Blair) bathed here during his time at Eton (circa 1919).

4. Cross road, then zig zag left and right to follow path alongside railway viaduct. The brickwork is flowering in places, with vegetation growing out of the interstices. Follow path over footbridge then go right at end along a tarred lane. In due course you will pass Eton College Golf Course and the white hemispherical dome of The Herschel Observatory. When the road splits, fork left towards Swimming Pool Cottages. Proceed through gate and along gravel path that skims the edge of a cricket pitch, with Colenorton Brook and the Performing Arts Theatre on the right. At end of field, keep ahead and follow footpath around rugby pitch. When the two sets of goal posts co-align, bear right and then left to follow broad gravel path under archway.

A cyclist follows the footpath alongside the railway viaduct, that carries the GWR line from Slough to Windsor.

5. The wall to your right leads the eye toward the red fluted chimneys and crenellated turrets of Eton College. Lupton's Tower and the honey-coloured pinnacles of the Chapel provide the iconic view. Follow path across park and bear left at junction. Continue over footbridge then fork right, when path splits across College Fields. A diverse selection of trees has been planted here; the only thing missing are plaques to aid identification. To your right the muddy waters of the Thames are visible again. When you reach a road, go right, then right again after 100 metres, along footpath and across the landing stage of a brown corrugated boathouse. Go through metal swing gate into field. Cross driveway bounded by two gates, before crossing wooden footbridge over The Jubilee River.

The honey-coloured pinnacles of Eton College Chapel, viewed from College Fields.

6. Go right to follow path under the Black Potts Railway Viaduct. Note the substantial support that has been added to strengthen the nine brick arches of the original Victorian viaduct. You might be fortunate enough to see a heron with rifled beak standing stock still near the foaming waters of the weir, waiting for fish. It's also worth pausing in this secluded place to take on board some refreshment, as you imbibe the roar of the weir. Proceed along the right hand edge of Datchet Golf Course along a lightly worn path that soon becomes a track. About 100 metres before the track ends, go right up a flight of steps to gain road. Go right along pavement and over the Thames via Victoria Bridge. Note the four half turrets on each side of the bridge which provide pedestrian refuges.

7. At the end of the bridge, bear right over the white railings (at the earliest opportunity) and down the slope to pick up the Thames Path again. Keep going with the Home Park on your left and the muddy waters of the Thames on your right. Pass under a railway bridge where the Thames begins to swing left. Notice the wooded island on the right (Romney Island) that will remain with you for most of the journey home.

Boatyard established in Windsor since 1983, located at Romney Lock opposite Eton College and offering full boatyard facilities, including boat sales.

8. Go through a swing gate (near Romney Lock), and follow the waymarked route through a boatyard. Soon the path becomes a tarred lane with a railway track running alongside it. When you reach a footbridge over the railway, go half right along a narrow fenced path (Romney Walk) which brings you out near the Boatman pub. Keep following the Thames until you reach the end of the walk (on Windsor Bridge).

Salmon-coloured September sunset over Windsor Bridge.

A bevy of swans on the Thames promenade near Windsor Bridge

WALK 4: Eton Town Trail

Start: Windsor Bridge; Start reference: SU 968772; length = 1 mile (1.75 km); this route follows part of 'The Eton Walkway' (an official guidebook is available from the Tourist Information Centre).

1. Proceed across Windsor Bridge and past the black information board describing The Eton Walkway. Permanent bronze markers (bearing Eton's coat of arms) are set in the tarmac to identify the route of the Walkway. Pass The George Inn and proceed up Eton High Street. It is hard to imagine that for many centuries, this long, narrow street once formed part of the main road from London to Windsor.

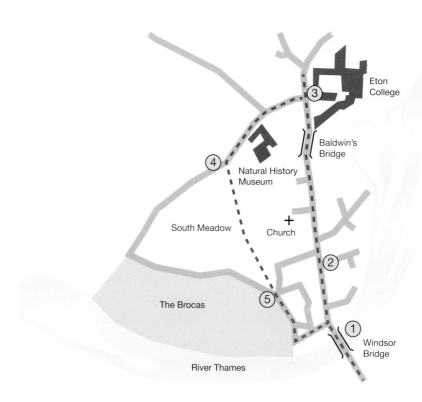

If you look above the shop fronts many of the first-floor buildings have flag poles which are flying the Union Jack. Pass the Eton Antique Bookshop and soon afterwards (on the right) you will notice a red pillar box, which is grade II listed, with an unusual vertical posting slot. Eton was the first village in England to have a post office and the name 'pillar' was derived from its fluted Doric decoration.

The Eton Walkway is a 2-mile circular walk connecting points of interest in the town and celebrating Eton's diverse community and rich heritage. 18 permanent bronze markers set into the ground identify the route and bear Eton's coat of arms.

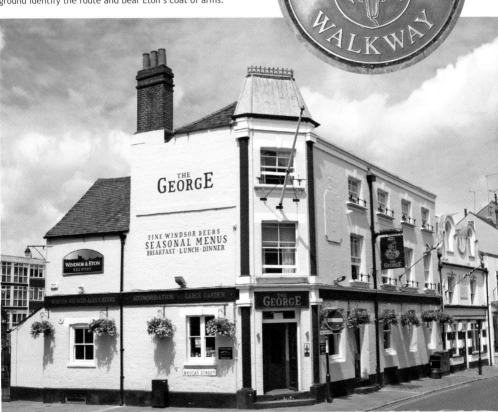

The George Inn, situated just across the pedestrian bridge in Eton, serves beer from the Windsor and Eton Brewery.

2. In due course a road leads off to the left, and the building with a turret and a copper-green cupola, is Baldwin's Institute, opened in 1912 and owned by The Baldwin's Bridge Trust. Maintain direction up the High Street passing the entrance to Eton College Health Centre and the church of St John the Evangelist (set back from the road). Pass Eton Library and Tom Brown Tailors, a bespoke tailoring service which makes clothing for Eton College boys. Cross Baldwin's Bridge, which was of strategic importance in Elizabethan times, since it crossed a tributary of the Thames and was on the direct route to London. A trust was set up to maintain it, and Bridgemasters were appointed to ensure its continued conservation and upkeep.

Above the shop fronts in Eton High Street are flagpoles flying Union Jacks.

Eton Health Centre (formerly called Eton Sanatorium).

Crossing Baldwin's Bridge with Eton College Chapel in the background.

A view of Baldwin's Bridge from the dried-up stream-bed that was once a tributary of the Thames.

3. Pass Eton College Chapel on the right, then proceed to the entrance of Eton College – probably the most famous public school in the world. It was founded by King Henry VI in 1440, who was scornfully described by his contemporaries as *'fitter for a cowl than a crown'*, and yet he was inspired to create something of lasting benefit to mankind. The College has been the Alma Mater of nineteen British Prime Ministers and has educated generations of British and foreign aristocracy (including members of the Royal Family) and sent forth a cohort of distinguished figures. Old Etonians, who became eminent writers include: George Orwell, P.B. Shelley, Aldous Huxley and Ian Fleming. Cross the road here and make your way towards a wrought iron Victorian lamp post (known as the 'Burning Bush'), which was once a favoured meeting point for Eton boys. Turn left here retracing your steps back along the Slough Road, then take the first right (at the lights) along Keate's Lane. You will notice here some of the Oppidan Houses used to accommodate Eton College boys (e.g. Hawtrey House). Keep ahead at the next bend along South Meadow Lane, passing Eton College Natural History Museum on your left, which is open to the public on Sunday afternoons, and the Music School. Keep going until you reach a building with a green roof (Eton Museum of Antiquities), with striking and original architecture, based on ancient Greek and Egyptian influences.

A view of Eton College Chapel from the cemetery.

Looking up at the honey-coloured towers and pinnacles of Eton College Chapel as a jet from Heathrow flies overhead.

4. Bear left here across the greensward, aiming for the opposite end of the sports field, just to the right of the Round Tower. The church tower on your left belongs to St John the Evangelist (the church you passed earlier). When you reach Meadow Lane car park, maintain direction through it (following the green tarmac paintwork).

5. Keep ahead along the road aiming for The Waterman's Arms and swing left, just before it, to join a road merging from the right (Brocas Street). Continue to Windsor Bridge, where the walk began.

Inn sign displaying a large fork and spoon outside The Waterman's Arms, Eton.

Looking across the pedestrian bridge that connects Windsor and Eton.

EPILOGUE

There is usually a story behind every book – a compelling reason for writing it, which has rarely anything to do with material gain; it inspires an author to draw upon numerous sources and to present the data he has unearthed in a creative and original way. My first encounter with Windsor dates back to 1986 when a distant relative (Gwen Shannon) informed me that an ancestor of mine, Richard Cope, was once the Chapter Clerk of St George's Chapel, Windsor Castle. Some family history research led me to conclude that he was in fact my great grandfather's uncle, and held office there in the late nineteenth century. His son, Francis John Cope, was born in Windsor and lived in Wraysbury, but later moved to Staffordshire in the late 1930s.[1] When Francis Cope died in 1947, his house and estate passed to my grandfather, Samuel Cope, who then lived in South Wales. How my grandfather heard about his legacy is a convoluted tale, and involved a chance encounter that nearly passed him by[2].

An oil painting of Richard Cope, Chapter Clerk, St George's Chapel, Windsor Castle (of unknown provenance), dating from around the 1870s.

Francis John Cope (1870-1947) and Richard Crosse Cope (1872-1893), sons of Richard and Anne Cope, 21 High Street, Eton and also the Upper Cloisters, Windsor Castle. Francis become a solicitor and lived in Wraysbury, before moving to Staffordshire. Richard (Crosse) attended Keble College, Oxford, and died at 6 Park Street, Windsor from Tuberculosis, aged twenty-one years. Photograph by Hills and Saunders photographers, Eton.

My father (Jack Cope) – then a young man of twenty-one – was dispatched to rural Staffordshire to investigate their new found inheritance. A year later, the entire Cope family left their council house in Caerphilly, South Wales and relocated to 'Ginger Croft' in Gnosall, Staffordshire. The house across the road (Fountain House) was owned by the Bancrofts, the village bakers, who lived there with their two daughters (Joan and Betty). In due course, my father made the acquaintance of their youngest daughter, Betty, and they subsequently fell in love and were married in December 1950. A few years later their first son – Michael John Cope – was born. At some point during my family history

A watercolour painting of Eton College from the Thames, by the artist William Evans (an Eton College Art Master), once owned by Richard Cope. It depicts Eton College Chapel, Lupton's Tower and College Fields in the early nineteenth century, with two gentlemen in the foreground preparing eel traps.

research, I had a light bulb moment: unless Francis Cope (Richard's son) had left his inheritance to my grandfather, my parents would never have met, and I would have never been born! The whole chain of events led me back to Richard Cope, Chapter Clerk of Windsor Castle, and I was determined to find out more about this remarkable man. Over thirty years later, my knowledge of his life is still incomplete, but a number of his belongings have since been passed on to me, including

an installation manuscript for a Military Knight, signed by the Prince Regent (George IV), and a quarto family Bible, published in 1639, and owned by Richard's grandfather. I unearthed letters written by Richard Cope to his father (John Cope), who lived in Tatenhill, Staffordshire. (Although the originals have been lost, the photocopies that remain piece together some of the family correspondence.) I was able to trace Richard's ancestry back ten generations to Sir Anthony Cope of Hanwell, Oxfordshire[3]. Census records and civil registration data show that Richard Cope lived at various locations in Windsor and Eton between 1861 and 1911, including 13 Peascod Street, 1 Alexandra Terrace (Grove Road), Eton College Cloisters, 21 Eton High Street, 6 Park Street and 2 & 4 The Cloisters, Windsor Castle. He also held office as Clerk to the New Governing Body of Eton College from 1872 onwards, retiring in 1901, with a pension of £100 p.a. He acquired many paintings, some of which were sold at auction on my aunt's death. A watercolour painting of Eton College from the Thames[4] by the artist William Evans (an Eton College Art master) appeared on 'The Antiques Roadshow' (Stafford) in 1991, and was valued at between three and five thousand pounds[5].

Richard Cope's obituary appeared in the Slough Chronicle on 14 June 1912, and here is an excerpt:

'We regret to record the death of Mr Richard Cope, formerly Chapter Clerk at Windsor Castle, which took place on Monday at his residence, 2, The Cloisters. The death occurred sadly through a fall downstairs the following Thursday, and the lamented gentleman expired on the Monday. Mr Cope had reached the age of 87 years and bore wonderfully his years. He entered the office of the Chapter Clerk sixty six years ago, and succeeded Mr Bachelor in the office of clerk nearly fifty years ago. At one time he held an equivalent office at Eton. He was greatly respected by all who knew him, and was a familiar personality in connection with St George's Chapel'.

The newspaper article goes on to say that his funeral took place at St George's Chapel after the usual morning service and a peal of bells was rung at The Curfew Tower. Richard Cope was buried at the Eton Cemetery[6] and, in addition to the family, a number of friends and sympathisers were present, including representatives from the Baldwin's Bridge Trust, of which the deceased was a member, and once held the office of Bridgemaster[7] (Chairman of the Trust).

Memorial brass plaque (inscribed in Latin) to Richard Cope, for forty-five years Chapter Clerk, St George's Chapel, Windsor; affixed to the lower wall of the Rutland Chantry, St George's Chapel, Windsor Castle.

To commemorate Richard Cope's time in office, a memorial brass plaque (inscribed in Latin) was later affixed to the wall of the Rutland Chantry, St George's Chapel, Windsor Castle. It contained the following verse from the Psalms:

'Lord, I have loved the habitation of thy house, and the place where thine honour dwelleth.'

Psalm 26:8

ACKNOWLEDGEMENTS

First and foremost, I would like to thank the numerous sources I have drawn upon to research this book, all of which are referenced in the detailed 'Notes' section. Certain books have been particularly influential and these are listed in the 'Select Bibliography'.

I am indebted to Doug Harding (Royal Photographer) for allowing me to use a number of his exceptional images of Windsor Castle and the Great Park and for his generous support of the project. His website and image bank can be found at: www.hardingphotographics.co.uk and www.theroyalboroughimagebank.co.uk Copyright acknowledgements are given in the relevant image captions.

I wish to thank Miss Charlotte Manley, CVO, OBE, Chapter Clerk, College of St George, for reviewing the section on St George's Chapel, and for useful discussions about Richard Cope. Thanks to the Dean and Canons of Windsor for kind permission to publish images of St George's Chapel.

I am grateful to Nick Day (Operations Manager of the Crown Estate) for giving approval to publish photographs of Windsor Great Park and for interesting discussions during the Heritage Walk around Windsor Great Park in 2018 (a Windsor Festival event).

Thanks to the Royal Collection Picture Library for guidance on photography within the precincts of Windsor Castle and for advising me on other contacts.

I am grateful to Windsor Library for the opportunity to browse back copies of 'Windlesora' in their local history section and to The Surrey History Centre (Woking, Surrey) for assisting me with family history research on Richard Cope.

My kind thanks to Richard Emeny (former Chairman of the Edward Thomas Fellowship) and The Edward Thomas Estate for providing the image of Edward Thomas.

Thanks also to Jo Farmer for looking over the section on 'The Upper Ward' and to Mr.Scan (www.mrscan.co.uk) for digitalising the family history transparencies used for the 'Epilogue'.

Finally, many friends and family have taken an interest in the project and offered support in various ways, and none more so than: Michelle and Mike Kerslake, Tom Harold, Sam Townsend, Alan Darley, Shona Wildman, Phil Simpson and Rob Cope.

SELECT BIBLIOGRAPHY

A detailed list of all books and websites referenced is given in the Notes section. The following books have had the most significant influence on the chapters relating to Windsor Castle, Windsor Great Park and Literary Windsor:

1. Rowse, A.L., *Windsor Castle in the History of the Nation*, (Weidenfeld and Nicolson, London, 1974)

2. Hill, B.J.W., *Windsor and Eton*, (B.T. Batsford Ltd, London, 1957)

3. Thomas, E., *Windsor Castle*, (Blackie and Son Ltd., London, 1910)

4. Marsden, J., *Windsor Castle Official Souvenir Guide*, (Royal Collection Trust, 2016)

5. Robinson, J.M., *Windsor Castle Official Guidebook*, (Royal Collection Enterprises Ltd., 2004)

6. Mackworth-Young, Sir R., *Windsor Castle, The Pitkin Guide*, (Pitkin Publishing, 2011)

7. St George's Chapel Guidebook 2017, (Dean and Canons of Windsor, 2017)

8. Bond, S., *St George's Chapel, Windsor Castle* (Pitkin Pictorials, 1973)

9. Wridgway, N., *The Choristers of St. George's Chapel*, (Chas. Luff & Co. Ltd., Slough, Berkshire, 1980)

10. Fielder, A., *Windsor Great Park, A Visitor's Guide*, (Copperhorse Publishing, Middlesex, 2010)

11. McDowall D., *Windsor Great Park, The Walker's Guide* (David McDowall, Richmond, 2007

12. Davenport, H., *Writers in Windsor*, (Cell Mead Press, Old Windsor, 1996)

NOTES

Introduction

1. Rowse, A.L., *Windsor Castle in the History of the Nation*, (Weidenfeld and Nicolson, London, 1974), p.9
2. Thomas, E., *Windsor Castle*, (Blackie and Son Ltd., London, 1910), p.5
3. Hill, B.J.W., *Windsor and Eton*, (B.T. Batsford Ltd, London, 1957), p.21

Chapter 1 Windsor Castle – A Tour of the Precincts

1. Robinson, J.M., *Windsor Castle Official Guidebook*, (Royal Collection Enterprises Ltd., 2004), p.5
2. See website: www.rct.uk/sites/default/files/Windsor Castle_Fact_Sheet.pdf 'Windsor Castle fact sheet' (accessed November 2018)
3. See website: www.britainexpress.com/articles/Castles/william.htm 'William the Conqueror's Castles' (accessed November 2018)
4. Mackworth-Young, Sir R., *Windsor Castle, The Pitkin Guide*, (Pitkin Publishing, 2011), p.6
5. Hill, B.J.W., *Windsor and Eton*, (B.T. Batsford Ltd, London, 1957), pp. 33-34
6. Thomas, E., *Windsor Castle*, (Blackie and Son Ltd., London, 1910), p.47
7. See website: www.rct.uk/event/conquer-the-tower (accessed November 2018)
8. Information given by the guide during the 'Conquer the Tower' tour in August 2018
9. See website: www.royal.uk/royal-archives (accessed November 2018)
10. Robinson, J.M., *Windsor Castle Official Guidebook*, (Royal Collection Enterprises Ltd., 2004), pp.11-13
11. Hill, B.J.W., *Windsor and Eton*, (B.T. Batsford Ltd, London, 1957), p. 96
12. See website: www.gutenberg.org: *The Diary of John Evelyn (Vol.2)*, 18th January 1671 (accessed November 2018)
13. Robinson, J.M., *Windsor Castle Official Guidebook*, (Royal Collection Enterprises Ltd., 2004), p.13
14. Robinson, J.M., *Windsor Castle Official Guidebook*, (Royal Collection Enterprises Ltd., 2004), p.14
15. Robinson, J.M., *Windsor Castle Official Guidebook*, (Royal Collection Enterprises Ltd., 2004), p.14
16. Rowse, A.L., *Windsor Castle in the History of the Nation*, (Weidenfeld and Nicolson, London, 1974), p.184
17. See website: https://en.wikipedia.org/wiki/Jeffry_Wyatville (accessed November 2018)
18. Thomas, E., *Windsor Castle*, (Blackie and Son Ltd., London, 1910), p.17
19. Marsden, J., *Windsor Castle Official Souvenir Guide*, (Royal Collection Trust, 2016), p.48
20. See website: www.royalacademy.org.uk/exhibition/charles-i-king-and-collector (accessed November 2018)
21. Robinson, J.M., *Windsor Castle Official Guidebook*, (Royal Collection Enterprises Ltd., 2004), p.19
22. Robinson, J.M., *Windsor Castle Official Guidebook*, (Royal Collection Enterprises Ltd., 2004), p.55

23. Marsden, J., *Windsor Castle Official Souvenir Guide*, (Royal Collection Trust, 2016), p.53
24. Mackworth-Young, Sir R., *Windsor Castle, The Pitkin Guide*, (Pitkin Publishing, 2011), p.14
25. Thomas, E., *Windsor Castle*, (Blackie and Son Ltd., London, 1910), p.16
26. Rowse, A.L., *Windsor Castle in the History of the Nation*, (Weidenfeld and Nicolson, London, 1974), p.16
27. Hill, B.J.W., *Windsor and Eton*, (B.T. Batsford Ltd, London, 1957), p. 30
28. Ashmole, *Order of the Garter*, (London, 1672)
29. Hill, B.J.W., *Windsor and Eton*, (B.T. Batsford Ltd, London, 1957), p. 35
30. Rowse, A.L., *Windsor Castle in the History of the Nation*, (Weidenfeld and Nicolson, London, 1974), p.24
31. Bond, S., *St George's Chapel, Windsor* (Pitkin Guide, 1973), p. 3
32. Hill, B.J.W., *Windsor and Eton*, (B.T. Batsford Ltd, London, 1957), p. 35
33. Hill, B.J.W., *Windsor and Eton*, (B.T. Batsford Ltd, London, 1957), p. 55
34. Rowse, A.L., *Windsor Castle in the History of the Nation*, (Weidenfeld and Nicolson, London, 1974), p.37
35. Rowse, A.L., *Windsor Castle in the History of the Nation*, (Weidenfeld and Nicolson, London, 1974), p.43
36. Mackworth-Young, Sir R., *Windsor Castle, The Pitkin Guide*, (Pitkin Publishing, 2011), p.14
37. *Garter Day Souvenir Guide 2018* (Dean and Canons of Windsor), p. 8
38. Robinson, J.M., *Windsor Castle Official Guidebook*, (Royal Collection Enterprises Ltd., 2004), p.12
39. Bond, M., *St. George's Chapel, Windsor, The Quincentenary Souvenir Book of Photographs* (Garden House Press, London, 1975), p. 27
40. See website www.gutenberg.org : *The Diary of John Evelyn (Vol.1)*, 8th June 1654 (accessed November 2018)
41. Bond, M., *St. George's Chapel, Windsor, The Quincentenary Souvenir Book of Photographs* (Garden House Press, London, 1975), p. 45
42. Bond, M., *St. George's Chapel, Windsor, The Quincentenary Souvenir Book of Photographs* (Garden House Press, London, 1975), p. 19
43. For further details see website: www.stgeorges-windsor.org (accessed November 2018)
44. Manley, C., *St George's Chapel Guidebook 2017*, (Dean and Canons of Windsor, 2017), p. 3
45. Wridgway, N., *The Choristers of St. George's Chapel*, (Chas. Luff & Co. Ltd., Slough, Berkshire, 1980)
46. See website for further details on becoming a Friend of St George's: www.stgeorges-windsor.org/friends-and-support/friends-descendants (accessed November 2018)
47. Rider, C., *St George's Chapel, Windsor Castle: An Illustrated History*, (Dean and Canons of Windsor, 2017)
48. Manley, C., *St George's Chapel Guidebook 2017*, (Dean and Canons of Windsor, 2017)
49. Brindle, S. (Ed.), *Windsor Castle: A Thousand Years of a Royal Palace*, (Royal Collection Trust, 2018)

50. Mackworth-Young, Sir R., *Windsor Castle, The Pitkin Guide*, (Pitkin Publishing, 2011), p.11

51. Hill, B.J.W., *Windsor and Eton*, (B.T. Batsford Ltd, London, 1957), p. 59

52. Mackworth-Young, Sir R., *Windsor Castle, The Pitkin Guide*, (Pitkin Publishing, 2011), p.11

53. Hill, B.J.W., Windsor and Eton, (B.T. Batsford Ltd, London, 1957), pp. 126-127

54. Thomas, E., *Windsor Castle*, (Blackie and Son Ltd., London, 1910), p.48

55. Mackworth-Young, Sir R., *Windsor Castle, The Pitkin Guide*, (Pitkin Publishing, 2011), p.11

56. See website: www.changing-guard.com/changing-guard-windsor-castle (accessed November 2018)

57. See website: www.thamesweb.co.uk/windsor/castle/guards.html (accessed November 2018)

Chapter 2   Windsor Town

1. Savage, R., *Windsor - Thomas Cook Pocket Guide*, (Thomas Cook Publishing, 2011), p.6

2. See website: www.victorianweb.org/sculpture/boehm/16.html (accessed November 2018)

3. See website: www. en.wikipedia.org/wiki/Small_Diamond_Crown_of_Queen_Victoria

4. See website: www.thamesweb.co.uk/royalty/queenvicstatue.html (accessed November 2018)

5. See website: www.harteandgarterhotel.com/about-us (accessed November 2018)

6. See website: www.thamesweb.co.uk/windsor/guildhall/guildhall01.htm (accessed November 2018)

7. See website: www.windsor-berkshire.co.uk/windsor-guildhall

8. See website: www.windsor.gov.uk/conference/the-windsor-guildhall-p232841 (accessed November 2018)

9. See website: www.windsor-berkshire.co.uk/the-crooked-house (accessed November 2018)

10. Kupfermann, E., *Windlesora No. 31*, (Windsor Local History Group, 2015)

11. See website: www.windsorparishchurch.org.uk/userfiles/file/Welcome_leaflet.pdf (accessed November 2018)

12. Savage, R., *Windsor - Thomas Cook Pocket Guide*, (Thomas Cook Publishing, 2011), p.37

13. See website: https://en.wikipedia.org/wiki/Windsor_%26_Eton_Central_railway_station (accessed November 2018)

14. See website: https://en.wikipedia.org/wiki/Windsor_Railway_Bridge (accessed November 2018)

15. See website: www.geograph.org.uk/photo/4429400

16. See website: https://en.wikipedia.org/wiki/Windsor_%26_Eton_Riverside_railway_station (accessed November 2018)

17. See website: https://windsorlink.co.uk/windsor (accessed November 2018)

18. See website: www.theatreroyalwindsor.co.uk/history.php (accessed November 2018)

19. See website: www.windsor.gov.uk/things-to-do/alexandra-gardens-p67873 (accessed November 2018)

20. See website: https://windsorlink.co.uk/windsor (accessed November 2018)

21. See website: www.stgwindsor.org/about-us (accessed November 2018)

22. Wridgway, N., *The Choristers of St. George's Chapel*, (Chas. Luff & Co. Ltd., Slough, Berkshire, 1980), p.96

23. Wridgway, N., *The Choristers of St. George's Chapel*, (Chas. Luff & Co. Ltd., Slough, Berkshire, 1980), p.97

24. See website: www.stgeorges-windsor.org/image_of_the_month/developing-st-georges-school (accessed November 2018)

25. Wridgway, N., *The Choristers of St. George's Chapel*, (Chas. Luff & Co. Ltd., Slough, Berkshire, 1980), p.108

26. See website: www.statista.com/statistics/373081/uk-royal-tourism-admission-numbers-by-establishment/ (accessed November 2018)

27. See website: www.windsor.gov.uk/visitor-information/statistics-and-data (accessed November 2018)

Chapter 3   Windsor Great Park

1. See website: www.windsorgreatpark.co.uk (accessed November 2018)

2. See website: www.windsorgreatpark.co.uk/en/live-and-work/the-local-area (accessed November 2018)

3. Fielder, A., *Windsor Great Park, A Visitor's Guide*, (Copperhorse Publishing, Middlesex, 2010), p.15

4. Hill, B.J.W., *Windsor and Eton*, (B.T. Batsford Ltd, London, 1957), p. 97

5. See website www.gutenburg.org : *The Diary of John Evelyn (Vol.2)*, 28th August 1670 (accessed in November 2018)

6. McDowall D., *Windsor Great Park, The Walker's Guide*, (David McDowall, Richmond, 2007), p.127

7. McDowall D., *Windsor Great Park, The Walker's Guide* (David McDowall, Richmond, 2007), p.129

8. Fielder, A., *Windsor Great Park, A Visitor's Guide*, (Copperhorse Publishing, Middlesex, 2010), p.71

9. McDowall D., *Windsor Great Park, The Walker's Guide* (David McDowall, Richmond, 2007), pp.108-109

10. See website: www.royalcollection.org.uk/collection/georgian-papers-programme/george-iii-notes-on-agriculture (accessed November 2018)

11. See DVD: *'The Madness of King George'* (2007) starring Nigel Hawthorne and Helen Mirren

12. See website: www.britannica.com/biography/George-IV (accessed November 2018)

13. McDowall D., *Windsor Great Park, The Walker's Guide* (David McDowall, Richmond, 2007), pp.108-109

14. See website: www.royal.uk/royal-ascot (accessed November 2018)

15. Vickers, H., *The Royal Mews at Buckingham Palace: Official Souvenir Guide*, (Royal Collection Enterprises Ltd., 2012), p.20

16. See website: www.rct.uk/visit/the-royal-mews-buckingham-palace/highlights-of-the-royal-mews#/#carriagehorses (accessed November 2018)

17. Hill, B.J.W., Windsor and Eton, (B.T. Batsford Ltd, London, 1957), p. 101

18. McDowall D., *Windsor Great Park, The Walker's Guide* (David McDowall, Richmond, 2007), p.49

19. Fielder, A., *Windsor Great Park, A Visitor's Guide*, (Copperhorse Publishing, Middlesex, 2010), p.91

20. Fielder, A., *Windsor Great Park, A Visitor's Guide*, (Copperhorse Publishing, Middlesex, 2010), p.90

21. Fielder, A., *Windsor Great Park, A Visitor's Guide*, (Copperhorse Publishing, Middlesex, 2010), p.108

22. See website: www.cumberlandlodge.ac.uk/about-us/what-we-do (accessed November 2018)

23. See website: www.windsorgreatpark.co.uk/en/live-and-work/guards-polo-club (accessed November 2018)

24. See website: www.guardspoloclub.com/smiths-lawn (accessed November 2018)

25. See website: https://en.wikipedia.org/wiki/Polo (accessed November 2018)

26. See website https://en.wikipedia.org/wiki/Polo_pony (accessed November 2018)

27. Fielder, A., *Windsor Great Park, A Visitor's Guide*, (Copperhorse Publishing, Middlesex, 2010), p.62

28. See website: www.bbc.co.uk/news/uk-england-berkshire-36012601 (accessed November 2018)

29. Hill, B.J.W., *Windsor and Eton*, (B.T. Batsford Ltd, London, 1957), pp. 104-107

30. Fielder, A., *Windsor Great Park, A Visitor's Guide*, (Copperhorse Publishing, Middlesex, 2010), p.35

31. Fielder, A., *Windsor Great Park, A Visitor's Guide*, (Copperhorse Publishing, Middlesex, 2010), p.39

32. See website: www. en.wikipedia.org/wiki/Fort_Belvedere,_Surrey (accessed November 2018)

33. McDowall D., *Windsor Great Park, The Walker's Guide* (David McDowall, Richmond, 2007), p.139

34. McDowall D., *Windsor Great Park, The Walker's Guide* (David McDowall, Richmond, 2007), p.148

35. McDowall D., *Windsor Great Park, The Walker's Guide* (David McDowall, Richmond, 2007), p.155

36. See website: www.thamesweb.co.uk/windsor/info/totem.html (accessed November 2018)

37. Sellars, R.W., *The Next Step in Religion*, (The Macmillan Company, New York, 1918)

38. McDowall D., *Windsor Great Park, The Walker's Guide* (David McDowall, Richmond, 2007), p.165

39. See website: www.visitsoutheastengland.com/things-to-do/the-savill-garden-p1148601 (accessed November 2018)

40. McDowall D., *Windsor Great Park, The Walker's Guide* (David McDowall, Richmond, 2007), p.142

Chapter 4   Windsor Events

1. See website: www.windsor.gov.uk (accessed November 2018)

2. See website: www.rwhs.co.uk/royal-windsor-horse-show-history (accessed November 2018)

3. See website: https://windsorfestival.com/about (accessed November 2018)

4. See website: www.runwindsor.com (accessed November 2018)

5. Davenport, H., *Windlesora No. 28*, (Windsor Local History Group, 2012), pp.31-34; also see website: www.windsorhistory.uk (accessed November 2018)

6. See website: www.royalwindsortriathlon.co.uk (accessed November 2018)

Chapter 5   Literary Windsor

1. Davenport, H., *Writers in Windsor*, (Cell Mead Press, Old Windsor, 1995)

2. Shakespeare, W. *The Merry Wives of Windsor*, (Penguin books, London, 2005). See 'Introduction' by Catherine Richardson

3. See website: www.nosweatshakespeare.com/play-summary/merry-wives-windsor (accessed November 2018)

4. Thomas, E., *Windsor Castle*, (Blackie and Son Ltd., London, 1910), p.52

5. Banerjee, J. *Literary Surrey*, (John Owen Smith, Headley Down, Hampshire, 2007), p.19

6. See website https://en.wikipedia.org/wiki/John_Evelyn (accessed November 2018)

7. See website www.gutenburg.org : *The Diary of John Evelyn* (Vol.1), 8th June 1654 (accessed November 2018)

8. Davenport, H., *Writers in Windsor*, (Cell Mead Press, Old Windsor, 1995), p.35

9. See website www.gutenburg.org : *The Diary of John Evelyn* (Vol.2), 18th January 1671 (accessed in November 2018)

10. Banerjee, J. *Literary Surrey*, (John Owen Smith, Headley Down, Hampshire, 2007), p.23

11. Davenport, H., *Writers in Windsor*, (Cell Mead Press, Old Windsor, 1995), p.47

12. See website www.gutenburg.org: Swift, J., *Journal to Stella*, Letter XXVII, July 31st 1711 (accessed November 2018)

13. See website www.gutenburg.org: Swift, J., *Journal to Stella*, Letter XXIX, September 1st 1711 (accessed November 2018)

14. See website: https://penandthepad.com/meaning-poem-windsorforest-22353.html (accessed November 2018)

15. Davenport, H., *Writers in Windsor*, (Cell Mead Press, Old Windsor, 1995), p.51

16. See website www.gutenburg.org ; Pope, A., *Windsor Forest*, 1713 (accessed November 2018)

17. Davenport, H., *Writers in Windsor*, (Cell Mead Press, Old Windsor, 1995), p.53

18. Fitch, E.L., *Windlesora No.5*, (Windsor Local History Group, 1986), pp. 26-30

19. Davenport, H., *Writers in Windsor*, (Cell Mead Press, Old Windsor, 1995), pp.123-127

20. See website: https://www.edward-thomas-fellowship.org.uk/ (accessed November 2018)

21. Hollis M., *Now All Roads Lead to France: The Last Years of Edward Thomas* (Faber and Faber, London, 2011)

22. Moorcroft Wilson, J., *Edward Thomas, From Adlestrop to Arras: A Biography*, (Bloomsbury, London, 2015) p.193

23. Thomas, E., *Windsor Castle*, (Blackie and Son Ltd., Glasgow, 1910)

Chapter 6   The River Thames

1. Jefferies, R., *The Open Air*, (Chatto & Windus, London, 1885). See also www.gutenberg.org for a free eBook.

2. Tellem, G., *The Thames*, (Jarrold Publishing, Andover, 2003), p.11

3. Atterbury, P. and Haines, A., *The Thames*, (Cassell Paperbacks, London, 2002), p.9

4. Davenport, N., *Thames Bridges from Dartford to the source*, (Silver Link Publishing, Kettering, 2006), p.28

5. Belloc, H., *The Historic Thames*, (J.M. Dent, 1909). See also www.gutenberg.org for a free eBook

6. Hall, S.C., Mr. and Mrs, *The Book of the Thames*, (Charlotte James Publishers, Teddington, 1859 and 1978), p.1

7. See website: www.frenchbrothers.co.uk/downloads/documents/w40minsouvenir.pdf (accessed November 2018)

8. See website: www.frenchbrothers.co.uk/downloads/documents/w2hrsouvenir.pdf (accessed November 2018)

9. See website: www.dorneylake.co.uk/home.aspx (accessed November 2018)

10. See website: https://en.wikipedia.org/wiki/Locks_and_weirs_on_the_River_Thames (accessed November 2018)

11. See website: www.bbc.co.uk/news/uk-england-berkshire-24771303 (accessed November 2018)

12. See website: www.thamesweb.co.uk/windsor/thames/locks_weirs.html (accessed November 2018)

13. See website: www.thamesweb.co.uk/windsor/windsorhistory/floods47.html (accessed November 2018)

14. See website: www.thamesweb.co.uk/floodrelief/relief_bckgrnd.html (accessed November 2018)

15. See website: www.bbc.co.uk/news/uk-england-berkshire-25727040 (accessed November 2018)

16. Peel, J.H.B., *Portrait of the Thames*, (Robert Hale, London, 1967), p.40

17. Davenport, N., *Thames Bridges from Dartford to the source*, (Silver Link Publishing, Kettering, 2006), p.112

18. See website: www.thamesweb.co.uk/windsor/windsorbridges/AlbertBridge2003.html (accessed November 2018)

19. See website: www.thamesweb.co.uk/windsor/windsorbridges/bridges2.html (accessed November 2018)

20. Beechcroft, G., *Windlesora No.32*, (Windsor Local History Group), pp. 21-22

21. Davenport, N., *Thames Bridges from Dartford to the source*, (Silver Link Publishing, Kettering, 2006), p.115

22. See website: www.thamesweb.co.uk/windsor/windsorbridges/winbridge.html (accessed November 2018)

23. See website: https://en.wikipedia.org/wiki/Windsor_Railway_Bridge (accessed November 2018)

24. Davenport, N., *Thames Bridges from Dartford to the source*, (Silver Link Publishing, Kettering, 2006), p.117

25. Davenport, N., *Thames Bridges from Dartford to the source*, (Silver Link Publishing, Kettering, 2006), p.118

Epilogue

1. Francis Cope's motives for moving away from London and the Home Counties are unclear, but the outbreak of World War II may have been a contributing factor.

2. My grandfather's friend (or neighbour) happened to see the following advert in the Western Mail in 1947/1948: 'To whom it may concern: S.G. Cope, last heard of, and believed to be living, in Caerphilly, South Wales, please contact Birch and Co., London, and you may hear something to your advantage'.

3. Public family trees (Cope-Morgan and Clark) on www.ancestry.com (accessed November 2018), indicate that Richard Cope's ancestry can be traced back ten generations to Sir Anthony Cope of Hanwell, Oxfordshire, who was knighted by Queen Elizabeth I in 1592–93 and granted a baronetcy by King James I on 29 June 1611. Parish records have yet to confirm this claim.

4. The painting was subsequently inherited by my aunt, Marjorie Berrow. On her death, this painting (together with the painting of Richard Cope) was sold at auction in Shrewsbury by her son, Richard. The current location of both paintings is unknown.

5. See website: www.youtube.com/watch?v=RfK9a2NY81Y (accessed November 2018): Antiques Roadshow, Stafford, 1991.

6. I have yet to locate Richard Cope's grave in any of the Eton Cemeteries (Eton Cemetery Chapel, St John the Baptist, Eton Wick or St John the Evangelist) despite numerous visits. According to Buckinghamshire Records Office, there is also no record of a monumental inscription to Richard Cope in the above cemeteries.

7. See website: https://sites.google.com/site/baldwinsbridgetrust/home/roll-of-bridgemasters (accessed November 2018) for a roll of Bridgemasters. Richard Cope served as Bridgemaster in 1890 and 1899.

Procession of landaus (convertible horse-drawn carriages) set out from Windsor Castle towards The Copper Horse en route for Royal Ascot.

INDEX

Aerial view of Windsor Castle and town from high above the river. © *Doug Harding*.